LITTLE BOOK OF

British 60's Music

Robin Bextor

LITTLE BOOK OF

British 60's Music

First published in the UK in 2014

© Demand Media Limited 2014

www.demand-media.co.uk

Printed and bound in Europe

ISBN 978-1-910270-04-2

Contents

The Sounds of the 60's
The British Top 40

It is amazing looking back to the start of the 1960's to see just how much has changed in that time. Of course there has been a huge technological shift since then-my Thank Your Lucky Stars annual for 1963 is produced by a TV station that no longer exists (ABC TV) and is full of references to "spinning discs" and when they mention a disc jockey it is a Pete Murray type (i.e. a middle aged man) usually wearing a suit or –heavens above- a roll neck sweater. Now the digital age means we will never see a programme like "Stars", "Top of the Pops" or "Ready Steady Go!" again. Never will clandestine hours under the bedclothes be spent listening to the like of Radio Luxembourg, Radio Geronimo or the pirate stations like Caroline.

Now we have access to everything, all the time. We don't even buy records now. And never will young people define themselves simply by what music they listen to. Keith met Mick on that railway platform in Dartford and became friends because they recognised the albums each was carrying, they knew they had an affinity.

But the whole of society has changed from those days and if you step back to

"What was special was that for a glorious and colourful short period of time, hardly a week went by without some new creative talent emerging on our airwaves"

the actual start of the decade in question-1960 - then the change is even greater because what we mean now by the 60's actually kicked off rather neatly right at the end of 1962 with the release of one 7 inch record "Love Me Do".

The advent of The Beatles and everything that followed on from them, meant that allied to changes in society such as (and in no particular order) the birth control pill, cheap foreign holidays, mass produced cars and televisions, satellite technology, the end of rationing, greater rights for gay people, women, children and the spread of good education for ordinary families, the power of the trade unions and a host of other landmark leaps of progress that the UK was ready for something special.

We became a different society from the class ridden, grey, economically humbled Britain of the 1950's. From gazing enviously across the Atlantic to our far richer

ABOVE
The original title screen for 'Top of the Pops'

cousins we suddenly were transformed into a nation of achievers and Worldbeaters. The British invasion, when our groups went over to the States and took their charts by storm, reset the balance - where The Beatles led, we were happy to follow as our empire grew based not on economic might but on wit, talent and style. The 1960's was the UK's decade and we enjoyed it, we drove our Mini's

down the King's Road, wearing flower power clothes, made great films, wrote great books, we won the world cup, the decade ended with Monty Python on top of the comedy world and our music was unrivalled.

What was special was that for a glorious and colourful short period of time, hardly a week went by without some new creative talent emerging on our airwaves, some new direction in music was created; something new to excite us was presented for our edification. Looking back at the charts week by week you realise that there was an explosion in song writing, a huge growth in people being interested in music and as a result some really great sounds were made.

In this book we have not tried to quantify that, or even order those bands and artists who helped to change our society and our way of looking at it, but have created a top 40 of artists that simply could not be ignored for what they did. Some of them barely had a hit at all-Pink Floyd for example had two top twenty singles in the decade but who could deny them a place in the top division?

We have also included only those acts that were either British or predominately

British-so Frank Ifield is left out as an Aussie whereas the Bee Gees who were born here and based here are in. There is no room for the Beach Boys or Roy Orbison because of their origins, and despite their undoubted influence we have had to omit the likes of Marc Bolan and David Bowie who have been deemed 70's artists, the Barron Knights and the Bonzo Dogs due to our lack of humour, and a slew of bands like Soft Machine, Caravan, King Crimson, Yes, Chicken Shack and Fairport Convention who although part of the landscape did not do quite enough by 1969 to warrant inclusion.

Then there are the shooting stars like Badfinger, Honeybus, Thunderclap Newman and others like them who were brilliant but are maybe for inclusion next time.

So that's the 40 artists. There is one other name missing from the main list, and that is the name that everyone would put top of the pile, the one group who every single person would assume is there and that, of course, is The Beatles themselves. And that's because they start this book because without them then the other 40 would probably not be here at all.

Robin Bextor

The Beatles

It is pretty much impossible to over emphasise the role of The Beatles in creating the amazing explosion that happened right across the Western World in the arts, and especially in music and in particular songwriting.

The 60's began in earnest on December 15 1962 when Love Me Do entered the UK charts and for the next eight years during the course of the decade we witnessed the transformation of just about every element of life socially, morally, politically and artistically. At the forefront of every sea change were the fab four as they became our cultural pathfinders picking a way through the ever increasing and ever more complex strands of philosophy, politics, artistic expression and showmanship that came our way.

The Mersey Sound wasn't created just in Liverpool but in Hamburg and it was a unique synthesis that made the Beatles. To begin with at its heart were John and Paul. Their story has become show biz legend- it began with a chance meeting at Woolton Parish Church on June 15th 1956, when McCartney who was 13 and just a couple of days away from his 14th birthday, was introduced to the leader of the schoolboy skiffle band-The Quarrymen-who were about to entertain the milling crowd at the church fete. He was John Lennon, a couple of years older, beer on his breath and a confident swagger in his step.

Now when you visit the church there

❝They represented a whole class and generation of young people who were baby boomers, who had grown up after the Second World War❞

The Beatles' hairstyles amd fashion sense brought them almost as much attention as their music

are souvenir reproduction fete programmes to buy as mementoes of that day, you can go on a Beatles tour (in fact several) taking in Mathew Street and what is left of The Cavern, ride on Beatles' buses and stay in Beatles' hotels. Buy Beatles mugs and T-shirts and photograph Beatles' statues. Visit their old homes, which have become National Trust memorials, walk down Penny Lane and look through the gates at Strawberry Fields. You can walk past LIPA, the academy Paul set up at the old art school and meet taxi drivers who can remember the Casbah, Mona Best (Pete's Mum), Bob Wooler (the Cavern DJ) Allan Williams (the first manager) and Brian Epstein and the other characters who populate the amazing story.

That chance meeting was the start of the greatest musical partnership the world has ever known. Between them Lennon and McCartney re-wrote the rulebook on how to create music and how to approach the whole business of music. But we often forget just how good they were. After recruiting the even younger George Harrison to the cause the boys practiced endlessly, they honed their skills; they soaked up the musical tradition that was

on their doorsteps and despite the hardships they encountered economically they came through it. They represented a whole class and generation of young people who were baby boomers, who had grown up after the Second World War in a Britain experiencing a grey rationing after losing an empire and a way of life. They were adventurous setting off for Hamburg when under the legal limit, and when they got there they embraced everything that city had to offer.

They were not afraid to befriend the avant-garde German art students they met, and soak up the cultural differences offered. They saw the prostitutes and the pills, the punters and the playboys. They played great long five hour sets, crammed full of every type of music and they immersed themselves in the music of the US GI's they met in Hamburg-the Blues music of the deep south, the great legends of John Lee Hooker, Carl Perkins, Chuck Berry, Little Richard and the rest. They came home because George was too young, played a storming gig at Litherland Town Hall at the end of 1960 that put them in the forefront of Liverpool bands, then returned for another stint in Hamburg.

It was that second trip that created the

LEFT
Before The Beatles...
John and Paul as the
Quarrymen play the
Rainbow Room of the
Casbah Club.
August 29th, 1959

Producer George Martin with the Beatles in April 1963 as they collect their first of many sales awards, this one for a silver disc for the 'Please Please Me' single

THE **BEATLES**.. LONDON PALLADIUM
ROYAL COMMAND PERFORMANCE.1963

real Beatles. Stu Sutcliffe. left the group to stay with Astrid and become an artist, Lennon and McCartney wrote songs and just became as tight as two could be, and George became the master guitarist. They came back penniless but wise - Hamburg had been their music college and university in one go, next was the Cavern, a brief recording session where My Bonnie was laid down-leading to a fan asking in the Nems record store for a copy. That lead its owner Brian Epstein to manage them…every step of this story is so well known and documented. He saw them in the Cavern one lunchtime and realised how they had now amassed a huge local following. Liverpool was ready for the Beatles- pretty soon Brian realised Britain was ready for them too. Fed on a diet of manufactured pop stars by bosses like Larry Parnes that had produced a production line of Elvis clones the UK was living on a diet of tin pan alley songs or US covers. All that changed virtually overnight.

The record industry finally caught up with what was going on, and thank goodness it was George Martin and his little comedy label Parlophone where they landed, because it gave the Beatles

Playing the Top Ten
Club during their
second Hamburg stint

OPPOSITE
The Beatles London
Palladium poster, 1963

a bit of room and a great collaborator. George Martin indirectly got Ringo on board just before the space rocket of success took off, and by then the country was ready. There were thousands of young, mostly men, up and down the country who wanted to be like them. They wanted to travel the world, to be in a family style gang, to be creative and to taste what the new powerful media of television was giving the Beatles-fame, real intercontinental fame and it was a tremendous draw. And through all this you have to remember that they were the first, when Love Me Do crept into the chart in December 1962 there were literally no other guitar/vocal groups on the chart-Cliff and the Shadows was the extent of what we knew. The Beatles' voices were the first regional and working class voices we heard on radio and on TV, they were funny, witty and irreverent and that became the fashion too. It was hip to be clever.

What happened next changed everything, because in less than eight months by which time Please Please Me, From Me To You and She Loves You had all hit number one, the chart was literally awash with new groups from all over the country. And what was more important,

like Lennon and McCartney people were writing and creating their own music.

The pace of the 60's was unrelenting. Everything was done for the first time-conquering the US, making films, writing every song they recorded, playing stadiums, pushing the boundaries of recording, designing their own record sleeves, and working in Abbey Road they created their own artistic environment. There was no limit to what they could achieve and that was the message the rest of the world got. All over the planet bands were formed, song writing became the norm and a wave of creativity, free thinking and freedom of expression swept through society. They were hard working too, and full of ideas. They spread their fame and their ability, but because of their roots and the incredible bonding that had been born in Liverpool and Hamburg they were able to respond to the enormous challenges for those short but glorious years.

Of course there were other things happening too, and they were deciphered through the music: the religious, political, ethical and moral questions of the time were addressed in their albums and also, through the media scrutiny the Beatles were put under. Their own lifestyles, dress

LEFT
The eruption of Beatlemania in 1963 ensured that never again would the public get as close to the group as this Swedish fan did in Stockholm on October 26th

Pattie Boyd takes a comb to her future husband's famous locks on the set of 'A Hard Day's Night'

Paul McCartney

John Lennon

"The decade was over, the group that defined the age had finished and now it was time for something else"

sense, even their hairstyles, all became part of our learning curve. And they were not found wanting. They grew and rose to the challenge and we travelled with them. It was a magical mystery tour.

Now of course there is an unrivalled body of work for us to discover and re-discover. They have sold more records than anyone else, their albums are the fastest selling in history (even the compilation Number One is the biggest selling-as each new generation gets into the Beatles), they have sold a billion units, had more platinum discs, more number ones, more more more. But the numbers are not what mattered-they are a part of it- but what really is essential is the quality of the songs and the work itself, and the journey it took us on.

Every genre of music they explored they excelled in-you want heavy then look at Helter Skelter, you want challenging lyrics try Tomorrow Never Knows, you want melody what about She's Leaving Home or Yesterday, you want social commentary here's Lady Madonna, Eleanor Rigby and A Day in the Life. Every artist in this book owes a debt of gratitude to the Beatles, they just made it possible. Before them there were no Working Class Heroes, the only escape from the factory was sport, and they gave everyone an opportunity.

The timing was perfect, the inventions like satellite technology, recording studios, TV and mass media, stadium amplification and so on all contributed to the revolution but without the huge good fortune of having supremely talented individuals at the heart of it, then the 60's would never have happened the way they did.

On December 31st 1970 as the decade drew to a close Paul McCartney entered a plea in the London High Court to have the Beatles dissolved. The decade was over, the group that defined the age had finished and now it was time for something else. But of course as Paul said A is for Apple, that is what is on page one of your first book, and you can only be the first just the one time. What a time it was.

Adam Faith

Adam Faith should really be in the sounds of the 50's book, because it was that decade that spawned his pre-Beatles career. But Faith, real name Terry Nelhams-Wright (he only found out he was double barreled when he applied for a passport-at school he was simple Terry Nelhams), was a grafter and actually had over 20 top 50 hits during the golden decade.

He was born in Acton, on a council estate, worked full time from the age of 12 delivering newspapers and began an apprenticeship as a printer. But with cockney guile he made his way into the film industry where he thought acting might beckon. He was right. He worked in film cutting rooms before getting a residency at the seminal 2 I's coffee bar in a skiffle group. He was spotted and got a gig on the 6.5 special TV show, where he teamed up with legendary film composer John Barry, and that lead to a recording contract. Despite the odd false start the combination of TV appearances and a winning smile, a self-deprecating sense of humour, and interesting vowel sounds gave Faith a fighting chance of success.

What Do you Want remains a classic British chart topper in 1959 and a long string of similar orchestrated singles followed. His work was always just the right side of being a novelty record, but deep down most people realised Faith was not really a musician although for a while he did give Cliff a good run for his

> "He was spotted and got a gig on the 6.5 special TV show, where he teamed up with legendary film composer John Barry, and that lead to a recording contract"

money. He had 20 consecutive top 20 hits from 1960 to 1963. As soon as Merseybeat struck Faith's days in the charts were numbered and as the 60's began in earnest it was as an actor and entrepreneur that Faith really shone. He managed Leo Sayer (Leo not so happy with the contracts it must be said) and then became an investment analysis where he made a huge amount of money (before losing it all again) but Adam Faith is best remembered as ITVs "Budgie" and the deadly manager to David Essex in Stardust. He was a good and convincing actor, and his own life contained as many twists and financial turns as any plot of Minder he might have turned up in. He used to hold court in London's Savoy Hotel running his office from a table in the River Room surrounded by grandeur that his youth had lacked. He died in March 2003, but packed a lot into those 63 years.

ABOVE Adam Faith LP cover artwork

The Animals

The Beatles came from Liverpool but The Animals had Newcastle written all over them. Gruff Geordie vocalist Eric Burdon made certain of that even if his roots in the North East were later to be rejected in favour of the psychedelic sunshine to be found in California. But that's later on.

To begin with there was Alan Price and his R and B outfit playing in a slightly seedy club owned by Michael Jeffrey; The Downbeat jazz club. A habitué of the club the young stocky Burdon joined the band, and the completed line up of Chas Chandler, Hilton Valentine, John Steel, Burdon and Price transmogrified into The Animals (either because of their appearance or it was close in mood to The Beatles). Jeffrey managed them and got them signed to EMI's Columbia label, and took them to London where they recorded in early 1964 a reworking of Baby Let Me Hold Your Hand (co written by Bert Russell who penned both Hang on Sloopy and Twist and Shout) called Baby Let Me Take You Home. It hit the top 30 rising to number 21 and was the perfect curtain raiser to House of the Rising Sun their next single and a worldwide smasherooney. Like "Sun" this was credited as arranged by keyboardist Alan Price that obviously made quite a difference to his royalty statements, and is also made all the more appealing by the unique vocal style of Eric Burdon. On bass Chas Chandler

❝On the coat tails of the British invasion The Animals struck it big in the USA, Ed Sullivan beckoned and House of the Rising Sun remains one of the great hits of the 60's❞

held down the sound augmenting the vibrant organ sound from Price, and although not writing their own material The Animals managed to sound fresh, rugged and original.

On the coat tails of the British invasion The Animals struck it big in the USA, Ed Sullivan beckoned and House of the Rising Sun remains one of the great hits of the 60's. For two years the band enjoyed chart success via a number of Mickey Most produced tracks. He was very smart with his choice of material for the band. They were usually blues classics from the likes of Nina Simone, (Don't Let Me Be Misunderstood) Sam Cooke (Bring It On Home To Me) and some great anti-establishment tracks like We Gotta Get Out Of This Place and It's My Life.

The former featured a unique bass intro from Chandler and pointed the way towards his producing future and also had a great performance from

ABOVE
Alan Price performing

Burdon who made the track his own. But it was also the first hit without Alan Price who had quit the band amidst no little amount of acrimony and a series of complaints about flying-which he hated. Pretty soon the entire band was falling to bits, with Michael Jeffrey's managerial skills leaving the group's finances in

The Animals during a period of chart success in the 60's

tatters and confusion. Chas Chandler quit to become a great producer and manager looking after a young American guitarist called Jimi Hendrix and later Noddy and the boys from Slade!

Meanwhile Eric Burdon reformed a band called Eric Burdon and the Animals and following the advice from his back catalogue got out of this place and ended up in San Francisco where he became an embodiment of the counter culture/hippy movement and recorded some great hits like San Franciscan Nights and Monterey teaming up with Andy Summers and Zoot Money from Dantalian's Chariot. A long trip indeed for a Geordie boy. The Animals remain one of the great exponents of British blues-interpreting the songs of the USA in a unique and instantly recognizable form and with House of the Rising Sun known now as the first ever folk rock hit. The song had been around since the 1930's, and was getting known through a live version performed by Bob Dylan who instantly dropped it after hearing the Animal's version. "Sun" was also remarkable as the first hit in the USA for a British Invasion record unconnected to the Beatles. Heady times.

The Bachelors

With their nicely pressed blazers and roll neck sweaters The Bachelors were unthreatening, harmless and essentially dull exponents of an easy going alternative to the Mersey beat that was shaking the charts

Full of Osmondesque smiles and effortless harmonies they covered show tunes from the 1920's with a charming and tuneful honesty that had naïve easy listening written right through them. Needless to say the BBC lapped them up as convenient and polite guests on the Light programme, Royal Variety performances and middle of the road entertainment shows. But despite the bland exterior the Irish trio had a charm that is undeniable- and no doubt a bland interior.

Originally from Dublin the founding members of the trio were the Cluskey brothers Dec and Con with John Stokes.

They were all in their mid teens when in 1957 they formed their first band together "The Harmonichords". They instantly tasted success via some TV appearances, including an Ed Sullivan Ireland special but no real record hits. The lads signed with Decca and Dick Rowe-the man who famously turned down the Beatles- told them to change their name to the innocent sounding The Bachelors. That was in 1960 and two years later they turned their homespun charm into chart topping record sales when they hit the big time with Charmaine, Diane and a series of old songs performed in a

THE BACHELORS

"They were on the radio so much it was virtually impossible to avoid them no matter how hard you tried"

smiling and inoffensive style. No less than 8 top ten hits and a collection of top 30 singles followed turning them into household names and soon they were on the radio so much it was virtually impossible to avoid them no matter how hard you tried. Their last top ten hit came in 1966 with a cover of Paul Simon's The Sound of Silence but the Bachelors were far from done. They moved into the cabaret circuit, and continued their run on BBC becoming all round family entertainers with some more covers- like Hello Dolly- and a good line in groan worthy jokes and extremely sleight banter.

In 1984 the Cluskey brothers split with Stokes, and then there were two lots of Bachelors doing the rounds. But it is impossible to scorn those melting harmonies of Diane. Those innocent days of the early 60's might be a long way off but it appears that there is always room for at least one band like The Bachelors especially in places like Great Yarmouth and Blackpool.

Bee Gees

Although this is meant to be the best British bands of the 60's, with some Irish ones like The Bachelors included, the Bee Gees are reckoned by many to be Australian but we thought that through their sheer contribution they have made it into the reckoning-but also they are British really don't you think?

The Bee Gees are effectively three brothers- Barry, Robin and Maurice who were born on the Isle of Mann to English parents. They then moved to Chorlton in Manchester where they formed their first skiffle group. Then in 1958 they took off for Australia to their Dad's former home. By 1960 they had a recording contract and a string of live shows under their belt. They gained the name of the BG's (one G to begin with) and had a minor hit but at the end of 1966 they caught a boat ride back to Britain, hired drummer Colin Petersen who had followed them over and they were set for stardom.

The man to make it all happen was Robert Stigwood, a close associate of Brian Epstein who was used to doing things his own way. He had worked with Joe Meek as an independent producer and was not afraid to spend to accumulate. He was not afraid of the long game either...and with the Bee Gees he was still working with their catalogue nearly 50 years later. He spent on a promotional campaign behind their first UK single New York Mining Disaster 1941, deliberately courting comparisons

with the Beatles. The result was airplay and press coverage leading to a top twenty record. The follow up To Love Somebody did even better but it was their third-Massachusetts that hit the number One slot and propelled them to the top league.

Those three part harmonies and a unique writing style cemented their position and despite times when they have gone out of fashion, or lost their way, the Bee Gees have become one of the greatest success stories in music industry history. After Massachusetts came World, Words, I've Gotta Get a Message to You, I Started a Joke and a host of others.

But of course the best was still to come. The 60's saw an experimental, talented but essentially uncool act that crafted great records, disco gave us undiluted pleasure and made the Bee Gee's one of the biggest selling artists of them all. Stayin' Alive, Night Fever, Jive Talkin, Nights on Broadway, You Should be Dancing, How Deep is Your Love, Tragedy….how many platinum songs can you write? They have sold over 120 million records.

What's more their records are part of a wider cultural impact-they are linked to shows, films, Grease, Saturday Night Fever, that have changed the world. Their songs have been recorded with success by everyone from their brother Andy to literally hundreds of other artists; it is a vast amount of work and a virtually unrivalled catalogue of hits, probably only Paul McCartney and Michael Jackson can lay claim to more. I think we are right to bags them.

Billy Fury

From 1959 to 1966 Billy Fury had no fewer than 26 chart hits; only the likes of Cliff and the Beatles had more. Remarkably before that he had worked in Liverpool as a docker and on a tugboat. But despite a career cut short by illness Fury cut an iconic figure, hero-worshipped by the likes of Morrissey and still an artist revered and loved.

Originally born Ronald Wycherley the young Billy Fury started piano lessons at the age of 11 and was soon writing songs. But at 14 his Dad got him a guitar and his love of music went off the scale, he was determined to be a star and although never a great guitarist he loved the feel of it, the sense that here was a prop for a performance.

At 15 he left school and joined Ellison's Engineering initially as a tea boy, then as a riveter. But he was never going to last in the ship industry and decided that show business was the way out. He was focused on finding a way to impress fame maker Larry Parnes who was in town on a tour featuring Marty Wilde .

Famously Ron auditioned in front of Parnes during the show's interval, who decided there and then to shove him out on stage, and see how he got on. The theatre loved him and Parnes signed him, changed his name and got him a recording contract.

Parnes reasoned that no one called Ron Wycherley stood a chance of becom-

> **"From 1959 to 1966 Billy Fury had no fewer than 26 chart hits; only the likes of Cliff and the Beatles had more"**

ing a rock star, so he called him Billy after the bandleader Billy Cotton, and Fury because Ron was the reverse of furious-he appeared so shy. Billy's first record Maybe Tomorrow went top twenty and Parnes had another star on his hands.

Once the hits started coming Billy Fury needed a backing band. One of the first to audition came from Fury's native Liverpool-the Silver Beatles featuring Lennon, McCartney and the rest but despite asking for Billy's autograph Lennon turned the job down when he was told he would have to drop Stu Sutcliffe his art school mate from the line up if they wanted to work for Billy.

Halfway to Paradise, Jealousy, I'd Never Find Another You, When Will You Say I Love You, and In Summer all made the top 5 but two things were working against Billy. Firstly his health had always been suspect and a heart problem caused him increasing trouble. Touring was a torture for him, he was frequently on the point of exhaustion and collapse and as the 60's went on his health became more of an issue.

Also, of course, the industry had changed. The Larry Parnes stable was looking dated and old fashioned, the likes of Joe Brown, Eden Kane, and Marty Wilde were on the way out and although Billy Fury was still in the charts as late as August 1965 he could see the writing on the wall. His erstwhile backing band were now the shape of the present and the future, and a quieter life in the country beckoned.

But the signs were not good for a long and happy retirement, the first problem was his desire to keep creating music which made him restless, and the second was that he had never really saved for that rainy day. In 1971 the rain came in a downpour with the need for open-heart surgery, and then Inland Revenue came calling for back taxes. In 1978 Billy Fury went bankrupt and five years later he was dead, his heart problems getting the better of him. He had always told friends that he would be lucky to make 30 so that pessimistic outlook was beaten but his life was still preposterously short.

"Once the hits started coming Billy Fury needed a backing band. One of the first to audition came from Fury's native Liverpool-the Silver Beatles featuring Lennon, McCartney and the rest"

Billy J Kramer and the Dakotas

If ever the power of the Beatles needed to be shown then it is in the career of Billy J Kramer with the Dakotas. Billy J became an example of how anything touched by the magic hand of Lennon and McCartney was guaranteed stardom in that golden period of the 60's.

Born William Ashton in August 1943 in the Liverpool suburb of Bootle, Billy was on the Liverpool scene of the early 1960's . But times were tough and Billy was about to take a job in Rugby for British Rail when he was spotted by Brian Epstein who was determined to increase his roster of stars. Epstein signed him up and thoughts of a career in the transport industry were put on the back burner.

Billy chose the name of Kramer at random from a phone book but it was said that John Lennon gave him the "J" telling him it sounded a bit harder and if questioned he could say it stood for Julian-the name John had already chosen as his son's name.

Whatever the strength of his name

Billy J. rode to the top of the charts on the coattails of the Beatles. His first massive hit was Do You Want to Know a Secret, although inferior to the Beatles' version it was too good for everyone else and on the Parlophone label, produced by George Martin he just couldn't fail. It topped the charts, then came Bad to Me, another Lennon McCartney special and I'll Keep You Satisfied. They all went top five.

Backed by the Dakota's –a band from Manchester who insisted on separate and equal billing but who never did anything else away from Billy, the act swept into the US where as part of the British invasion Billy rose to stardom. The power and extent of the fame created in those short few months simply can not be over emphasized, this was a major phenomena and a life changing time for people like Billy J. But time was running out on him.

Billy's judgment could be a bit suspect. He was offered another McCartney song for his new release, but he chose to turn down Yesterday. Instead he came up trumps with a cover version of a song called Little Children, it gave him his biggest hit, but by now Epstein was losing interest in Billy and realised the Beatles

needed every ounce of attention he could give them. Two smaller hits followed but the peak had been crested.

The hits dried up but not Billy J. He split with the Dakotas and suffered from self-confessed problems with alcoholism. Billy has had no more hit records, but he turned things round, cleaned up and is now settled in the USA.

Cat Stevens

Cat Stevens is actually the second name (of three) to be used by Steven Demetre Georgiou, because now, of course, he is known as Yusuf Islam. At just 18 after playing around the London folk scene he impressed ex-Springfield Mike Hurst who produced his first album and got him signed.

The debut single I Love My Dog went into the top twenty, Mathew and Son released on December 30 1966 went to number two in the first weeks of 1967 propelling the album up the charts. John Paul Jones of Led Zep fame played bass on the tracks, and Here Comes my Baby (later a hit for the Trems) as featured in the Rushmore soundtrack is also track listed. An indicator of the singer-songwriter's potential the album is a minor classic-his next single was I'm Gonna Get Me

A Gun. Funnily enough we never learn what Mathew and Son actually did, but we do know we would not like to work there. From this record onwards Cat must've known his days of working in his family's restaurant were over.

Just as he has had three names then Cat's career falls pretty neatly into three phases. Phase one could be described as the early years of pop. After "Gun" he released A Bad Night which just grazed the charts but his days of working with Hurst were drawing to a close. He was after a more honest, less orchestrated sound and he achieved it after a long bout of illness by stripping everything down in collaboration with producer Paul Samwell Smith (of Yardbirds fame) and guitarist Alun Davis who became his lifelong collaborator. The result, phase two if you like, was the folk rock album Mona Bone Jakon (1970), which spawned the classic Lady D"Arbanville which went on to sell over a million copies and broke Cat in the USA.

Next up was Tea for the Tillerman the following year, which featured the brilliant Wild World and Father and Son. Cat Stevens was now recognised as a major global artist, which each subsequent album through the seventies cemented. Teaser and the Firecat gave us Peace Train, Moonshadow and Morning has Broken and each album took his success to a new level.

That is until 1977 when he converted to Islam took on his third name-Yusuf Islam and gave up the music industry. Then in 2007 a short 30 years later, enter phase three, when he released the first of two albums under his current name.

That's only three; they do say a cat can have nine lives.

> **"playing around the London folk scene he impressed ex-Springfield Mike Hurst who produced his first album and got him signed"**

Cilla Black

Like Billy J. Kramer, Cilla Black owes her music career to the Beatles and Brian Epstein because here is another example of the Merseybeat invasion of the charts. But where Cilla differs is in her incredible and sustained television career.

Cilla started life as Priscilla White, and only a journalist's error changed things. Bill Harry of Liverpool music magazine the Merseybeat reviewed her performance at a coffee bar calling her Priscilla Black and Cilla loved the name so it stuck. Her big break came when she started looking after the cloakroom at the Cavern where the resident band was The Beatles. They liked her and John in particular thought Brian Epstein should sign her as his only woman singer. The audition with the Beatles giving her backing was a disaster, they played in the wrong key and Epstein hated it....but Beatle John persisted and she was signed soon after.

For her first single Paul and John wrote Love of the Loved for her and it was a hit (of course). Her second single released at the start of 1964 was Anyone Who Had A Heart, it was a huge number one and Cilla was a star in her own right. The song by David and Bacharach was followed by You're My World which also hit the top spot. It's for You, Alfie and Don't Answer Me were highpoints as Cilla maintained her pre eminence amongst the UK's female singing talent-but increasingly Cilla was looking for other ways to entertain us. Cabaret was lucrative and all very well but Cilla really connected on TV. The first hints of reality TV were seen on some of her early shows, and her easy relaxed style added to her sense of humour ensured her status as a national treasure.

Best of all she had Beatles for friends and Paul wrote the theme tune for her-the brilliant Step Inside Love- which gave her another chart hit and a great start to the show.

As the 70's began Cilla scored again with Conversations and Something Tells Me. In all some 17 hits during the 60's and a clutch later on makes Cilla our most popular female artist of the decade, and don't even mention Surprise Surprise or Blind Date.

> **"Her big break came when she started looking after the cloakroom at the Cavern where the resident band was The Beatles"**

9

Cliff Richard and the Shadows

Throughout seven decades Cliff Richard together with the Shadows have been an ever present on the popular music scene, together and individually they hold a unique place in our showbiz landscape.

Now Sir Cliff, the boyish singer who was born Harry Webb in October 1940 is beyond criticism, and even compare because simply there is no one else remotely like him. He has had more hits; more acclaim and has created a reputation beyond even his wildest dreams when back in 1958 he released his first record.

John Lennon said that when Cliff had his first hit with Move It, that it marked the beginning of rock in Britain. Since then Cliff and The Shadows have had well over 130 records in the charts, have had almost 20 number ones but more than just statistics he has become "Cliff" an institution in our national psyche that stands for good humoured excellence, for honest to goodness pop and a status usually only reserved for

"First record with the new line up was Living Doll which went to number One"

the most popular members of the Royal family. He is simply untouchable.

It is hard to conceive today that when he started out there were elements of British society who saw him as edgy, and even slightly threatening.

He was born in Lucknow in India in October 1940. His father worked for the Indian Railways in catering and his mother at a school. In 1948 when India became independent the family came back to the UK by boat, and from living with servants on the edge of Calcutta, they found themselves in a council house in Cheshunt. As a teenager young Harry became interested in skiffle and his Dad bought him a guitar when he was 16.Harry formed a five piece singing group before playing in the Dick Teague Skiffle Group.

Within a year or two Harry was fronting a band called the Drifters and had changed his name to Cliff Richard-

Cliff to sound hard and Richard as a tribute to Little Richard the US rocker. In the late 50's there was a clamour for a home grown Elvis type and a number of contenders entered the ring: Cliff with his dark good looks and quiff certainly fitted the bill and that first record with Move It as the "A" side went to number two.

In July 1959 things changed slightly but significantly for Cliff. The Drifters became the Shadows (they could not have kept that name with the US version so pre eminent) and with a line up of Hank Marvin, Bruce Welch, Jet Harris and Tony Meehan behind

him Cliff Richard was ready for a new softer sound that became his own. No longer just an Elvis impersonator Cliff became, well…CLIFF.

First record with the new line up was Living Doll which went to number One, Travellin' Light did the same and the 1960's started with Expresso Bongo from the film of the same name in the charts. Meanwhile the Shadows-who had their own recording contract with EMI as well, hit number one with the great instrumental Apache. Even when Jet Harris and Tony Meehan left the Shads to record two great songs-Diamonds and Scarlett O'Hara on their own-the "brand" was not dented.

In this way a pattern was set, Cliff and The Shads frequently topping the charts with great toe tapping melodies, The Young Ones, Do You Want to Dance, Bachelor Boy, Summer Holiday, On the Beach, In the Country and on and on while The Shadows would chip in with Kon-Tiki, Wonderful Land, Dance On, Footapper, Atlantis… all great instrumentals with fabulous catchy tunes and often a dance move or step to go with them. Unbeatable.

What's more Bruce Welch and the boys would often write songs for Cliff, so the machine was self-perpetuating.

And in concert things worked well too, the Shadows would close the first half of the show with 30 minutes of their hits before Cliff would return for a 45 minute rendition of his songs. Together they were terrific, and the songs were finely honed and caught just the right atmosphere of the times.

The strange thing about Cliff and the Shadows as well is that the rise of the Beatles seemed to make little difference to their appeal. Like everyone else they had to respond (and in fairness The Shadows as a group had a waning pop-ularity) but unlike many they were far from washed away in the wake of Beatlemania. They were too far ensconced in the scene to be dented, in fact Cliff found a new audience of slightly older fans who just stayed with him-and he repaid them with hits throughout the 60's-including Eurovision, TV shows, and of course a string of innocent loveable films featuring Melvyn Hayes or Richard O'Sullivan for comedy, Una Stubbs for glamour and dance and Cliff for being just Cliff. Summer Holiday is still a classic.

And so it continued for not just the 60's but for 50 years. Sir Cliff might have failed to become as big in the USA as he is here (although We Don't Talk Anymore and Devil Woman both sold over a million there) but otherwise every possible goal has been reached, every milestone passed, every showbiz record broken or equaled. He might not write his songs, he might not get down and dirty with the Stones, he might not smash his equipment but Cliff has become something else. An institution, a man with an amazing back catalogue and an artist who is the best Cliff it is possible to be.

10

The Dave Clark Five

They called it the Tottenham sound to rival the Mersey sound and for a month or so it seemed that the Dave Clark Five could be real contenders with the Beatles

They were the second band to go over to the US as part of the British invasion and played the Ed Sullivan Show straight after the Fab Four, In February 1964 The Beatles had appeared for three weeks running and the DC5 did the next two. They even knocked the fab four off the number one position the previous month when I Want to Hold Your Hand was replaced by Glad All Over. They also neatly fitted into the 60's with the final line up for the Dave Clark Five coming together in 1962 and they disbanded at the end of the decade.

The Five were really all about Dave Clark as their name suggests. He effectively managed the band, produced the records, chose the records and wrote and owned the songs. In fact he was ahead of the game in this respect as he was the first pop artist to understand the importance of owning his own master recordings. No wonder he was glad.

But to begin with after leaving school with no qualifications at 15 in 1957 Dave became a stuntman, appearing in over 40 films. He put his earnings towards buying a drum kit, and teaching himself how to play it, and then hiring a studio for a recording session. Com-

"The Five were really all about Dave Clark as their name suggests. He effectively managed the band, produced the records, chose the records and wrote and owned the songs"

ing from Tottenham, he was a Spurs supporter and his initial aim was to earn enough money from his new skiffle group's gigs to be able to follow his team to Holland for a tour.

After a number of formation changes and name swaps the group settled into being the Dave Clark Five and the line up was Dave on drums, Mike Smith on keys, Lenny Davidson on lead guitar, Rick Huxley on bass and Dennis Peyton on sax. By now they had quite a following especially amongst the mods of North London and they signed to EMI with Dave keeping those master rights up his sleeve.

After a couple of false starts they were placed on the Columbia label and they hit the jackpot in November 1963 with the release of Glad All Over. Dave Clark sat grinning out from a million black and white TV sets as he belted out the driving beat surrounded by his boys all dressed in matching polo necks and jackets, smart slacks and shiny shoes.

They were even bigger in the US than here, topping the charts, selling out the Carnegie Hall and getting mobbed. Just like The Beatles they made their own movie, Catch us if You Can was directed by John Boorman and was a decent piece of work but Dave realised acting wasn't for him. But no matter, Bits and Pieces was massive and they followed it with no less than a further 15 top 40 records in the States, 13 of which charted in the UK. In all they appeared 18 times on the Ed Sullivan TV show.

But after four years the carnival was over and the hits began drying up. By 1970 the band was finished and Dave Clark thought about other things. He was well prepared, in addition to owning all of the DC5 catalogue he also acquired the rights to Ready Steady Go! The best music show of the 60's and he sat on those assets for the next few decades. In addition he devised and put on the musical Time starring Cliff.

The DC5 were inducted into the Rock and Roll Hall of Fame, but sadly three of the five are no longer with us. Now Dave can still be seen driving his Rolls around the West End from time to time, but he is a great example of capturing the moment, the energy of the 60's and turning that moment to his full advantage. And no one can dispute they made a couple of truly great records.

Dave Dee Dozy Beaky Mick and Tich

1961 and five friends from sleepy Salisbury in Wiltshire decide to form a band. They hold down residences in Hamburg and Cologne where they get their act together.

Four years later when back home they have a shot at the big time, Joe Meek the famous producer sets up a recording session with them, but despite their best endeavors it all goes horribly wrong culminating in Meek throwing his cup of tea against the wall and storming out. His assistant enters the shell-shocked recording studio to tell the band "Mr Meek will not be continuing with the session". But it actually turns out for the best…

Because from there Dave Dee and the Bostons come into contact with songwriters Ken Howard and Alan Blaikley who immediately suggest changing their name to Dave Dee, (really David Harman former policeman) Dozy (Trevor Leonard Ward-Davies) Beaky (John Dymond) Mick (Michael Wilson,) and Tich (Ian Frederick Stephen Amey) and they start writing some songs for the band.

February 1966 and Hold Tight becomes

the first top ten hit for DDDBMT the first of no fewer than 14 hits for the band .

Dave eventually became a magistrate and most notably helped found the Nordoff Robbins charity. He died in 2009 and weirdly when a PC Dave had attended the death car crash of Eddie Cochrane. And as for the other names-well apparently they were their genuine nicknames

The follow up to Hold Tight Hideaway is from the same team of songwriters Ken Howard and Alan Blaikley and was released in June 1966 spending six weeks on the chart and getting to number 10.

At their funniest when trying to be

straight faced, songs like The Legend of Xanadu and Zabadak were never meant to be taken seriously and there was always something of the pantomime about the group. Lots of cape action and stomping about was the order of the day, combined with those catchy melodies from the team that also launched the Herd with Peter Frampton to stardom.

Last Night in Soho saw them catch a small element of the hallucinogenic times but really they remained as anachronistic as possible, always more end of the pier than Woodstock. The Wreck of the Antoinette allowed for some pirate outfits and that seemed more appropriate.

At the end of the decade they had run out of steam, Tich could still do his "funny look" but the industry had changed and Dave Dee was able to head off to Magnet Records as a record executive where I remember working with him on a Bad Manners video. A lovely charming bloke, with a gappy smile and a load of great stories.

BELOW
Dave Dee, Dozy, Beaky, Mick and Tich in 1967

Donovan

Donovan started out as a little becapped Dylanesque figure with a line in whimsical protest songs and grew into a major artist pushing the folk song into areas of psychedelia, Celtic rock and unusual narrative.

He was born in Glasgow in 1946 into a working class background, where he contracted polio as a small child that left him with a limp. In 1956 the family moved to Hatfield and at 14 he began playing guitar surrounded by folk music, which his family loved. He enrolled as an art student but soon dropped out and hit the road, where he played guitar on street corners, met buskers and after playing with folkies like Mick Softley developed a unique finger picking style.

Pye recorded a demo with him and his influences ranging from Woody Guthrie to Ramblin' Jack Elliot were obvious.

In 1965 the links with Dylan were strengthened. With Bob touring the UK, as seen in the film Don't Look Back, Donovan was an almost constant part of the entourage especially during an extended sequence shot in the Savoy Hotel where they partied. It was here that he first met the Beatles and it was also here that he took part in one of rock video's most famous moments when he helped write and make the cue cards for Dylan's iconic Subterranean Homesick Blues video in the back alley of the hotel.

By now Donovan had a couple of good songs in his repertoire: Colours and Catch the Wind, both in that protest song mold but with an inner beauty and subtlety. They charted and the singer then began a fruitful partnership with one of the 60's most prolific and successful producers Mickey Most.

Most had a great ear for the music hook and he brought out the best in Donovan. Colours was followed by the sparkling Sunshine Superman, and then the cosmic Mellow Yellow, There is a Mountain and Jennifer Juniper-all beautiful classic melodies at once both naïve and knowing. Donovan went to Rishikesh with the Beatles to meet the Maharishi, where he introduced them to the guitar sound he loved and it surfaced on the White Album. He came back from India full of songs and one of the first boxed set double albums came partly from them-A Gift from a Flower to a Garden, a double album that was both childlike and trippy, with some terrific tunes of course.

Most worked his magic again by taking Donovan into slightly heavier territory with Hurdy Gurdy Man-which was also written in India (which became a classic Steve Hillage number) His last hit of the 60's, following Atlantis, was Babarabbajagal (Love is Hot) which paired Donovan with Jeff Beck-a masterstroke from Most as it provided one of the most unlikely combinations of the decade but was simply brilliant.

Since the 60's Donovan has not troubled the charts but his songs are an eternal catalogue of the mood of the time and show the artistic and relative sensitivity that was fostered at that time-something that modern music does not reflect in the mass market-but his influence is still strong and plenty of singer songwriters from this decade could do a lot worse than write songs like Jennifer Juniper or Mellow Yellow.

I met Donovan by chance a couple of years ago in Los Angeles when we were staying in the same hotel in West Hollywood and both had gone onto the roof garden to watch the July 4th fireworks in the night sky. Donovan went back to his room and returned a few minutes later with his guitar and for half an hour played in this surreal setting for my wife and children while we sat cross-legged under the glittering sky listening to Wear your Love Like Heaven. That is 60's magic.

LEFT
Donovan pictured on 12th July 1965, just 19 years of age

Dusty Springfield

Dusty was born Mary O'Brien in West Hampstead in London on April 16 1939 into a musical and eccentric Anglo-Irish family. She joined a trio in the late 50's called the Lana sisters (no sisters, she answered an ad in The Stage to audition) after a period of singing in folk clubs with brother Tom. But the sisterhood wasn't for her and soon after in 1960 she and Tom (real name Dionysius O'Brien, he was a real brother) together with Tim (real name Reishad Field, no relation) formed a folk trio and standing in a field in Springtime at that moment decided to call themselves The Springfields both collectively and individually. They went to Nashville to record an authentic folk album but even as early as this Dusty (so called because she was quite a tom boy) was struck by how much she loved the emerging pop/soul/blues sound.

The Springfields were instantly successful with their catchy songs-Bambino, Island of Dreams and Say I Won't be There were all hits -and Dusty's eye catching looks. They even had chart success in the USA in the same sort of style as Peter, Paul and Mary.

But Dusty had her darkly eye shadowed gaze on other musical styles and although Mike Hurst had now joined the trio instead of Tim, she felt restricted by the Springfields basic folk

"For four years running Dusty was the top female vocalist in Britain, she was hugely popular in the US and not just as a singer. She produced her own sessions and understood the importance of writing her own material"

base. Tom went off to write and produce The Seekers and Dusty set off on a solo career. So in late 1963 Dusty recorded I Only Want to be With You, by Ivor Raymonde (father of Simon-a Cocteau twin), and it instantly sounded a classic. Horns, r n' b rhythms, backing singers it was everything The Springfields were not and far closer in style to the US girl bands that Dusty had heard earlier in the decade. The result was a million seller, a chart hit on both sides of the Atlantic and an appearance on the first ever Top of the Pops. Dusty was a solo star.

She followed it with Stay Awhile, and then another classic: I Just Don't Know What To Do With Myself. She allowed her extravagant hand gestures and postures to come to the fore, in interviews she was funny and disarming- she was simply Dusty and her fans loved her.

For four years running Dusty was the top female vocalist in Britain, she was hugely popular in the US and not just as a singer. She produced her own sessions and understood the importance of writing her own material-even if it was only a B-side. Her choice of material was unerring as well, great tunes like Goin' Back, I Close my Eyes and finally those brilliant Memphis sessions.

By the end of the 60's she looked to expand what she was doing, she signed to the label of her heroine Aretha Franklyn-Atlantic Records-and with the likes of Tom Dowd came up with what is still regarded as one of the best female vocalist albums of them all- Dusty in Memphis. Although something of a misnomer because she finally re-recorded her vocals in New York the album contained a richness in sound and material that was unrivalled. Son of a Preacher is still revered to this day.

That was the highpoint of her career really, a brief return to the charts came with the Pet Shop Boys in 1987 with What have I done to Deserve This? But Dusty preferred her slightly lower profile existence. Questions about her sexual orientation had become boring and intrusive, and in 1994 she was diagnosed with breast cancer. She died in 1999.

She leaves a great legacy, a catalogue of delicious TV appearances often with her sense of humour to the fore, some delightful live shows, and a record archive brimful of great melodies, lovely arrangements and that voice.

Englebert Humperdinck

Englebert was born Arnold George Dorsey on 2 May 1936 in Madras, India one of ten. He moved to Leicester some ten years later and his first brush with music of any note came playing the sax in nightclubs. He soon started singing and his first single came in 1958-I'll never Fall in Love Again , but it was to be nearly ten years later before Englebert emerged and he tasted fame.

After suffering from TB Dorsey met up with old mate Gordon Mills in 1966. Mills was now managing Tom Jones. Mills suggested a name change…to Englebert after the 19th Century German composer and a new recording deal was set up with Decca. In February 1967 Englebert became the name on everyone's lips. "Release Me" hit number one on both sides of the Atlantic - it remains his biggest and best known smash. It spent over a year in the charts.

His strange looks and easygoing style won Eng. fans, they were called Hump-

erdinckers, and two more ballads There Goes My Everything and The Last Waltz, which along with Am I That Easy To Forget and A Man Without Love all went top Three. It meant Humperdinck was indelibly written into the national psyche.

By the end of the decade Englebert had ten top twenty hits and the 70's yielded another six. But the big bucks for Eng.

were in cabaret now, and he moved to California where those dollars were available just down the road in Vegas. He has continued making music over the years, he represented the UK in Eurovision in 2012 coming 25th (out of 26). But that's not how we will remember Englebert; it is as the side boarded smoothie on stage singing Release Me in his bow tie and tux.

Fleetwood Mac

Probably the most unlikely candidates for international superstardom Fleetwood Mac were formed in 1967 in South West London in the middle of the British Blues explosion. The band was centred on the mercurial talents of Peter Green, guitarist extraordinaire.

Green had followed the golden line of guitar greats to strum centre stage for John Mayall and his Bluesbreakers. He had replaced Eric Clapton in the line up, and like Clapton his time had come to leave the worthy but less commercial offerings of the Bluesbreakers for the bright lights and strobe effects afforded by the rock stage. He saw what Clapton was achieving with Cream and set out to experience music in a less controlling structure.

The line up of the Bluesbreakers he left was essentially the early Fleetwood Mac but with the addition of John Mayall himself on keyboards, as Fleetwood Mac was based on the rhythm section of drummer Mick Fleetwood and Bassist John McVie. Green recorded a few tracks with Fleetwood and McVie and decided it was worth a go, but McVie who was old even then, wanted the security of the Bluesbreakers, after all he was on £20 a week and was planning to get married to Christine Perfect the keyboardist and vocalist with Chicken Shack. Incidentally she was also UK female vocalist of the year and a terrific talent.

Green combined to create the mystical Albatross, an instrumental that took the band to the top of the charts. Fame and international success, based essentially on those blues based albums, meant that the band was on the road and in a state of flux. Label changes followed (they even flirted with the idea of joining the Beatles' Apple label as Mick Fleetwood was George Harrison's brother in law!) but two great singles cemented their eternal fame: Man of the World and Oh Well both went top three in 1969 and Fleetwood Mac were in the envious position of being artistically credible-able to share the bill with the likes of Ten Years After and also selling loads of singles and albums. The USA loved them, Europe the same, what could possibly go wrong?

The answer of course was everything. Peter Green was increasingly unwell and unstable mentally. As the sixties came to an end the effects of mind bending drugs and being surrounded by some strange characters took its' toll. Green became increasing schizophrenic and his last recording for the band was the amazing Green Manalishi (With the Two Pronged Crown) which stormed the charts as well. The live Boston tea party

After much coming and going eventually Green got his way and the new band recorded what could have been a Blues-breakers album in early 1968, very earnest Blues covers and originals with the trio augmented by Jeremy Spencer. Two stand out tracks from that album (which dented the charts at 4) were Black Magic Woman and Need Your Love so Bad.

Their second album released later in 1968 was in the same vein but the band had grown. Danny Kirwan came in on guitar and Christine Perfect added some keyboard sounds. Kirwan and

(Feb 1970) version is simply incredible.

But that was Green's swansong; he felt pretty strongly that the band should give all their money away and some of the other band members felt differently rather strangely. In the summer he quit, returning to Richmond and a little house where he could be seen for years after pottering around, not missing the big time at all. Meanwhile his band members were in a total state of transition and confusion, with label changes galore, fresh starts, re-starts and financial confusion. Spencer told the band he was popping out for a magazine and never returned, Perfect joined full time, Kirwan was sacked. Album followed album in the early to mid seventies with no cohesion, despite some lovely moments and creative songs-especially from Christine McVie as she was now called. There was even a time when the band's manager took an alternative group on the road as Fleetwood Mac as he was so exasperated with his real group's antics, fall outs and affairs.

And that would have been that for the Mac if it wasn't for the fact that they went on to become the world's biggest band. It was of course all by chance. In 1974 Fleetwood Mac-or what was left of them were based pretty much in the States, their days of being a hard core British r n' b outfit fading fast. While in the studio Mick Fleetwood heard a record by an American duo called Buckingham and Nicks. Fleetwood realised Lindsay Buckingham could play guitar, sing and write, he was the answer to their prayers. Fleetwood offered him a job straight away in the band and Buckingham accepted on the condition that his partner Stevie Nicks could come too.

The result the following year was a fresh start really-they called the album Fleetwood Mac and it had tracks such as Rhiannon (from Nicks) and Over My Head and Say You Love Me (from Christine McVie). It sold 5 million copies. The Mac had arrived.

The next year the entire band experienced personal problems, divorces, affairs, drug troubles…it was great for song writing! In 1977 the result was Rumours, and it sold 40 million copies. There they were the most chaotic band in history back at the top of the charts. Peter Green still plays the blues with his Splinter group. He really did give all his money away by the way, and I went to school with someone who got given his guitar.

Freddie and the Dreamers

Freddie was Freddie Garrity, an ex milkman who gave up the milk round when Merseybeat came a calling. He was actually from Manchester and together with Bernie Dwyer, Pete Birrell, Derek Quinn and Roy Crewdson (the Dreamers) they signed to EMI in the wake of Love Me Do. They soon found themselves on the same bill as the Beatles touring the country and even "borrowed" one of the Beatles songs a cover of the James Ray tune If you Gotta Make a Fool of Somebody.

It must have been tiring being Freddie, he was forever jumping around, hurling his 5ft 3in frame across the stage, running about in circles and pulling a variety of funny faces. But to tell you the truth he was charming and funny and provided much needed light relief amongst the endless stream of boy bands the beat explosion threw up. Not only that but he was a charming bloke and it must have been lovely being a dreamer.

They concentrated their chart success

into a brief 18 month period which kicked off with the aforementioned "Fool" which had been a cover version anyway, its' just they did it exactly like The Beatles did… but then who wouldn't. Their best song was next I'm Telling You Now which was co-written by Freddie and it hit Number One in the US as well being a big smash in the UK during the summer of 1963.

Come November and they followed it up with the equally catchy You Were Made For Me which they hilariously played around with for their album title which was called You Were Mad For Me. I still like that joke.

The following year saw three more hits, Over You, I Love you Baby, and I Understand but by Christmas they had peaked and the only way was down. They continued to have some success in the US , a TV series Little Big Time, and Do the Freddie was a hit in America as well. But we tired of that loveable man with the big

glasses, tight trousers and frantic antics and around 2000 Freddie and the Dreamers stopped performing live.

Freddie Garrity died in 2006, he was 69.

"To tell you the truth he was charming and funny and provided much needed light relief amongst the endless stream of boy bands the beat explosion threw up"

Georgie Fame

Georgie Fame holds a unique position amongst the 60's hit makers. He had three top ten hits and all of them went to number one. But Georgie was far more than just a hit maker; he played a seminal role with a whole generation of music makers and continues to exert a major influence today.

He was born Clive Powel on June 26 1943 in Lancashire and after working briefly in a cotton mill (remember we used to have some industry then) he became an entertainer at Butlins in North Wales.

At just 16 years of age he moved to London where he joined the Larry Parnes stable playing backing fro Billy Fury. Parnes gave him his new name and he fronted a backing band called the Blue Flames. When Billy Fury got rid of the band Georgie kept them going and they became regulars on the blues scene. Fame developed into an excellent piano player with jazz, ska and reggae influences and the Blue Fames got a record deal. They also appeared in 1964 on Ready Steady Go with Georgie now behind a Hammond organ with that distinctive Booker T. sound rolling around.

They were cool and "part of the scene" and it was only a matter of time before they hit a bigger audience. At the end of the year they released Yeh Yeh on the Columbia label and it hit the top of the

charts. Either with the Blue Flames or as a solo artist Georgie then had a run of hits lasting for most of the middle years of the decade: his next big hit Get Away was also a chart topper. 1966 saw Sunny light up our World Cup winning year and the following year The Ballad of Bonnie and Clyde also hit number one.

Later on Georgie teamed up with Alan Price and again had success with Rosetta but throughout the 70's, 80's and 90's Fame found work as a top rated sideman for the likes of Eric Clapton, Van Morrison and became a founder member of Bill Wyman's Rhythm Kings. An undoubted musical great Georgie Fame continues to play and was there at Cornbury this summer.

"They were cool and "part of the scene" and it was only a matter of time before they hit a bigger audience"

18

Gerry and the Pacemakers

Gerry Marsden is Liverpool through and through. His rendition of You'll Never Walk Alone is the cue for Liverpool supporters all over the world to get up and sing the anthem, in memory of Hillsborough and to commemorate that great City. There is no one more Mersey than Gerry.

It all started with the Beatles of course, but Gerry was on an equal footing with the fab four to begin with. Along with his brother Fred, Les Chadwick and Arthur Mac they ran them a close thing in the North West. They went to Hamburg, played the Cavern and when the Beatles signed to Brian Epstein, so did Gerry and the Pacemakers. When the Beatles signed to EMI so did Gerry, to Columbia though-not Parlophone. But George Martin still produced them. He suggested they record as their first single a song that the Beatles had worked on but not decided to put out. Gerry agreed.

Then in quick succession How Do you

Do it (March) I Like It (June) and You'll Never Walk Alone (October) were all released and all went straight to number one. No one had ever done that before.

Gerry had a great smile, a broad accent and was genuinely lovely to everyone who met him. He started writing and the hits kept coming-Don't Let the Sun Catch you Crying, Ferry across the Mersey, I'll be there. They hit it big in the US as well but there was one snag.

Unlike the Beatles the Pacemakers did not have the ability to change gear and move ahead of the curve and by 1966 the Pacemakers disbanded with their best days behind them. But Gerry is still around, making music and appearing on TV. He has made a couple of great charity records helping the cause. Put simply everyone loves Gerry.

19

Herman's Hermits

Herman, real name Peter Noone, had been a child actor even appearing on Coronation Street as Stanley Fairclough, but at just 15 he signed up for the Hermits leaving the Rover's behind him. In the charts every year from 64 to the end of the decade their first hit was the number One I'm into Something Good and the last hit of the 60's for them was My Sentimental Friend.

They were Herman's Hermits to begin with but the Manchester band became Herman and the Hermits for the main part of their run of success. At one stage they even rivaled the Beatles for popularity, especially in the US, and were regularly mobbed, screamed at and had locks of their hair stolen. The majority of this success was down to one man-Mickie Most.

Most produced virtually everything Herman and Co put out and it meant both a steady flow of hits usually found by Most, but also stopped the band writing as much as they might have done (they did write plenty of material, it's just Mickie Most had control of output and used songs by tried and tested writers) which eventually lead to their demise. But that was not until they had enjoyed the fruits of the British invasion. Signed to Most and through him to Columbia in 1964 Something Good was followed by Silhouettes, Wonderful World, A Must to Avoid, Mo Milk Today (written by 10cc's

Graham Gouldman) There's a Kind of Hush, and finally My Sentimental Friend in the summer of 1969.

Every one of those hits was accompanied by toothy Herman beaming at us from our TV sets in a smart suit, surrounded by his Hermits who embodied personable clean cut living and other parent loving qualities. They were the one band on Top of the Pops your Granny loved, just before she started hurling abuse at the Stones or the Animals. And they repaid that trust with Mrs. Brown You've Got a Lovely Daughter and a straightforward well-mannered approach to everything they did.

Which was surprising given the fact that Most controlled them rigidly. They were competent musicians but he insisted on hiring in session players for most of their songs and did nothing to let the Hermits expand into other musical areas. But then why change a winning formula. Herman eventually settled Stateside, where he still is today-a truly huge star from the 60's when middle America embraced him and the Hermits as the acceptable face of the British invasion.

The band disbanded in 1970 and the following year Peter Noone had a minor solo hit with Bowie's Oh You Pretty Things, with the thin white duke appearing on piano. He now lives in California.

The Hollies

Like Herman and the Hermits the Hollies were from Manchester but unlike the Hermits their musical credibility was never in any doubt, they contained some terrific talent from the word go. Only a handful of artists enjoyed more weeks on the charts in the 60s than the Hollies and few rivaled their three part harmonies, great guitar sound and catchy song writing.

The group started life as a duo featuring Allan Clarke and Graham Nash who were schoolboy friends. In the late 50's they went out as Ricky and Dane Young singing skiffly sort of things without a lot of success. At the end of 1962 they teamed up with another local band and called themselves the Hollies by August of the following year the line up had settled down to Clarke and Nash plus Tony Hicks, Bobby Elliott on drums and Eric Haydock. They were signed to EMI and the hits started: Stay, Here I go Again and Just One Look were all recorded with the settled line up and they all went top ten.

The Hollies represented the Manchester wing of the British invasion although their impact on the US was a little less frenetic than their Liverpool contemporaries. There was something unique about their music-mainly due to the harmonizing of their three way vocals. Hicks, Clarke and of course Nash were brilliant vocally and created an instantly recognisable signature sound.

In 1965 they scored their first Number One with I'm Alive. Later that year Look Through Any Window written by Graham Gouldman was their break through top forty hit in the States. Bus Stop written by the same composer the following year gave them their first top ten US hit.

But all was not completely fine in the garden. Management issues, in fact money, was causing problems especially with Eric Haydock who quit over missing sums. Bernie Calvert stepped in to replace him and increasingly Clarke, Nash and Hicks were now writing for the band so the degree of influence they had on their own music increased.

After the upbeat Bus Stop the band followed it with Stop Stop Stop, On a

"There was something unique about their music-mainly due to the harmonizing of their three way vocals"

Carousel, Carrie Anne and the brilliant King Midas in Reverse, which was a watershed moment with the Hollies. Although critically lauded the single under performed, and Graham Nash was not happy. He wanted to push the band into more challenging areas musically; the other lads were not ready for that yet.

As a commercial response he and Clarke wrote the anodyne Jennifer Eccles which duly did the business but when the other Hollies decided that an album of Dylan covers was next on the agenda Nash had had enough. He left the UK for the sunny climes of California, fell in with the Laurel Canyon chaps and blissed out on the Marrakesh Express with Stephen Stills and David Crosby, and was later joined by Neil Young. Not bad for the boy from Blackpool.

Meanwhile the other Hollies plus new boy Terry Sylvester finished the decade on a high with two top three records: Sorry Suzanne and He Ain't Heavy He's My Brother which was to become a recur-

ring hit. It featured Elton John on piano by the way as did their next hit- I Can't Tell the Bottom From the Top. But now it was Clarke's turn to get frustrated and in December of 1971 he quit the band.

The Hollies arranged a new vocalist and set off on the road only for their record company to release an old back catalogue number Long Cool Woman in a Black Dress featuring Clarke. It became a worldwide hit and Clarke was back in the band in 1973. The following year it was all worth it when another massive international hit The Air that I Breathe smashed into the charts.

In 1988 He Aint Heavy was number One again after being used in a commercial. It showed that over all those years no one had lost faith in the Hollies and that they were still loved by the record buying public. In 2000 Allan Clarke hung up his microphone but the Hollies have officially never split up and some of those early members still tour from time to time. Over 30 chart-hit singles means it's a great evening every time.

The Jimi Hendrix Experience

Jimi Hendrix was an American born artist, but the Experience were a London based band and their three studio albums – all for the Who's Track Records label-and five hit singles were all primarily UK releases with the band made up at least with 66% of Brits. Hendrix shone brilliantly but briefly-he accomplished everything in a startling four-year period

The Experience formed in London in September 1966. Hendrix had been a sideman in a number of US blues outfits, playing for the Isley Brothers and Little Richard amongst others. He was spotted by Chas Chandler of The Animals who brought him back to London, produced him and managed him, changed Jimmy to Jimi and set up the trio around his amazing guitar skills.

On drums was the jazzer Mitch Mitchell and on bass Noel Redding. With Dylanesque bubble perm hair, psychedelic clothes and a super loud amplified sound using distorted feedback and extensive wah-wah the Experience would have been

"The experience were more than just a vehicle for Hendrix, collectively they created an amazing sound"

amazing to watch, mind-blowing to listen to. Along with Cream they pioneered the heavy power trio as a new form, with the virtuoso guitar at its core. Clapton and Hendrix almost instantly became soul brothers and on the night of Hendrix's death Clapton was on his way to see him with the gift of a new guitar. The death shattered Eric.

Hendrix was born in Seattle in 1942 within days of arriving in London, with his new band with him, they played the Scotch of St James club on October 19 1966,before going into the studio to rehearse and record. The result was the single Hey Joe that came out just before Christmas. On January 11, 1967, the band conquered London when they appeared at The Bag O'Nail's club. In attendance that night were John Lennon, Ringo Starr, Paul McCartney, Kevin Ayers, Brian Epstein, Lulu, The Hollies, the Small Faces, Pete Townshend, John Entwistle, Mick Jagger, Brian Jones, Donovan, Georgie Fame, Denny Laine, Terry Reid, Eric Clapton and Jeff Beck in fact everyone who mattered. Clapton rarely missed any of Hen-

drix's London gigs. Townshend is quoted as saying " Jimi changed the whole sound of electric guitar and turned the rock world upside down". Clapton was blown away "after Pete Townshend and I went to see him play, I thought that was it, the game was up for all of us, we may as well pack it in." The following week the record entered the charts rising to number 6.

But the experience were more than just a vehicle for Hendrix, collectively they created an amazing sound, Mitchell with his background with Georgie Fame and jazz added subtlety and explosive fills, Redding (who had been a guitarist before) added a surprisingly simple but melodic bass line. They were instinctively in unison able to support long improvisations, and incendiary solos.

In all 3 great studio albums came out on Track Records during this time: Are you Experienced? Axis Bold as Love and Electric Ladyland recorded in New York. All went platinum both sides of the Atlantic with Ladyland hitting the US number one spot. There were five hit singles Hey Joe, Purple Haze, And the Wind Cries Mary,

Burning of the Midnight Lamp and All Along the Watchtower.

In June 1969 the band dissolved, with relationships fracturing and drugs inevitably taking a toll. But by then they had cemented Jimi's reputation as the greatest guitarist we would know. They played Monterey Pop at their peak in 1967, outraged Lulu's fans with an impromptu version of Sunshine of Your Love when Cream split up, and rocked the Fillmore. Hendrix played around with a number of related combinations without Redding, but it is as the Experience he created his best work.

By the following summer Hendrix was dead. A confusing chaotic final few weeks saw him play the Isle of Wight festival, a couple of aborted European gigs and then return to London where on September 18, 1970 in a Notting Hill hotel room he was found dead, asphyxiated.

A Blue plaque is on the house he shared in Brook Street with Kathy Etchingham, next to the Handel museum but his real legacy is those three albums together with live recordings from Monterey and Woodstock where he provided one of the key moment of the decade. Both Redding and Mitchell were not destined for old age both dying in the first decade of this century.

The Kinks

In this strange world of show business there are few certainties but one thing is definite; everyone knows that Ray Davies is a bona fide genius. Anyone who writes such classic, individualistic and idiosyncratic songs as Days, Dead End Street, Autumn Almanac and Lola not to mention Waterloo Sunset just has to be one.

Raymond Douglas Davies (Born June 21 1944) and his brother Dave (b. February 3 1947) fought like cats and dogs and were the rocks on which The Kinks were built, along with drummer Mick Avory who lasted longer than most, and a pretty much revolving door of bassists and keyboard players. The Kinks more than anyone else managed to capture a sense of what it was really like to live in England during the post war period.

Davies was able to smile at the depressing back to backs, the loss of Empire, the landscape of characters and eccentrics that made up our society, from the aristocracy lazing by their pool to the fashionistas in Carnaby Street. He was the cornerstone of Brit Pop and the sensitive voice singing out for the individual, he spotted our nostalgia, and ridiculed our prejudices.

The brothers were born in North London, the youngest of 8 with 6 elder sisters. The family soon moved to Muswell Hill where the boys dropped anchor and still have their recording studio. At home they were immersed in a variety of music

RIGHT
The original line-up in 1965. From left: Pete Quaife, Dave Davies, Ray Davies, Mick Avory

from their parents' music hall to the jazz and rock n roll of their sisters. There were loads of parties at their home, and fighting too. It was lively.

Both brothers learned the guitar and they played skiffle together. At school with Pete Quaife they formed a band that played some local bars, they even had Rod Stewart as vocalist at one stage.

In 1962 Ray went off to Hornsey College of Art, yet another music great who attended art school. When he dropped out the band was reformed and they managed to get a couple of managers. In 1963 Larry Page became a third and producer Shel Talmy began working with them and Pete Avory joined as drummer. The ingredients were all there.

Around this time they changed their name to The Kinks, probably because of Dave's long hair and their slightly strange dress sense. Talmy got them a contract with Pye. The blue touch paper was lit.

The first two singles, Long Tall Sally and You Still Want Me failed to take off, but their third was a game changer. You Really Got Me. The pressure was on; the band had been told that Pye would drop them if they did not have a hit by the release of their third single. Ray was determined to get it right. He insisted on spending some time getting the sound perfect-Dave sliced his amp and speakers to dirty the sound, and came up with an entirely new r n b sound that laid the basis for every heavy metal and punk track that followed. It was the first record to be based on power chords. You Really Got Me was a classic and hit number one on both sides of the Atlantic.

Released in August 1964 it was everywhere that summer, and the follow up All Day and All of the Night was another Ray Davies special. That and Tired of Waiting for You, which came out at the beginning of 1965 were all chart toppers. The early hits were simply ground breaking and without the Kinks bands like the Ramones, the Damned, the Pistols and the rest would never have happened

The rest of the year the hits kept com-

❝Probably due to their fiery stage performances with tales of violence peppering the on the road stories, the Kinks were banned from touring the USA when the British invasion was at its' height❞

ing until December when they released Til the End of the Day. It was to be the last in this vein of power chord based rock songs before Davies became more whimsical, experimental and even more successful creating some of the greatest moments in the pop canon. It was actually the preceding record See My Friends that paved the way. Davies had written that after a fleeting trip to India, and marks a move towards the unique snapshot, slice of life, style songs that were to follow.

Their hits over the following two years included Dedicated Follower of Fashion, Sunday Afternoon, Dead End Street and Waterloo Sunset, Death of a Clown (released as a Dave solo), Autumn Almanac and Days, the 70's brought Lola, Apeman, No More Looking Back, Come Dancing any one of which would have confirmed Davies' reputation as a musical legend.

Probably due to their fiery stage performances with tales of violence peppering the on the road stories, the Kinks were banned from touring the USA when the British invasion was at its' height. By the mid 70's this was over turned and they were able to enjoy a second wave of success as a powerful arena rock band. But with such a catalogue of brilliant songs, concept albums like Village Green and Arthur in their locker the Kinks were always going to be destined for British Legend status. And so it is.

ABOVE
The Kinks on the the television program 'Fanclub' in 1967. From left to right, Ray Davies, Mick Avory, Pete Quaife, Dave Davies. Ray plays a Fender acoustic guitar and Dave his signature Gibson Flying V

Lulu

Marie McDonald McLaughlin Lawrie was born on 3 November 1948 in Lennox-town and grew up in Glasgow, where from the age of just 14 onwards she was known in Scotland and all over the world as simply Lulu.

A red headed ball of energy Lulu stormed into the UK charts while still under school leaving age with the powerful Shout in the summer of 1964. Lulu's career was kick started by one of pop's few women managers Marion Massey.

Massey's brother Tony Gordon owned a nightclub the Lindella in Glasgow where the young Marie Lawrie sang every Saturday night when aged just 13. Massey signed her up, changed her name to Lulu and that of the backing band to the Luvvers. She got Lulu a contract with Decca and set about finding her a hit record.

They found the ideal song on an old Isley Brothers record and moving Lulu into her family house in London where Marian Massey set about getting Lulu into the papers and onto TV. Soon the diminutive schoolgirl was a regular on shows like Ready Steady Go! a welcome contrast to the endless parade of boy bands, and backed by the Luvvers she belted out her hit alongside some other r n b classics.

That could so easily have been that for Lulu, but Massey was shrewd and her husband Mark, a writer and producer,

took her into musical areas that created an amazing career for the young Scot. They dropped the Luvvers and put Lulu together with Mickey Most. She had seven consecutive hits with Most, and a US number 1 with the title track from the movie To Sir with Love which she appeared in.

The 60's came to a close with Lulu winning the Eurovision Song Contest, which after Sandie Shaw and Cliff put her in great company. Boom Bang A Bang was the title and has become a by word for Euro excesses but Lulu never really seemed uncool, she married Maurice Gibb and ended the decade as part of pop's elite. The years after have been kind too. She has had numerous TV shows built round her, recorded with everyone from Elton John to Take That and David Bowie and still has that humour, charm and energy that we all loved way back then.

ABOVE
The diminutive Lulu with the big voice and bags of energy!

Manfred Mann

If one band captured the sound of happening swinging London in 1964 it was Manfred Mann, which was strange because really he wasn't from London at all.

The band started life as the Mann-Hugg Blues Brothers with Manfred Mann (who was a real person, with a beatnik beard and glasses, not just the name of the band) on keyboards and Mike Hugg (curly hair, no glasses) on drums. Manfred was actually from South Africa and having arrived in England threw himself headlong into the Blues craze washing over London and the south. It was a tidal wave with clubs and venues cropping up all the time and bands like the Rolling Stones, the Yardbirds and Graham Bond following guru's like Alexis Korner in discovering the roots music of the deep south of America.

Hugg and Mann assembled a band of like-minded muso's that included vocalist Paul Jones, Mike Vickers and later Tom McGuiness-a great line up. In March 1963 they signed to HMV and after a couple of very bluesy singles their big break came the following year when they were asked to provide the theme music to a new TV show on ITV. The show was Ready Steady Go! And it was a phenomenal success, becoming required viewing every Friday night when the weekend started right there. The theme song was perfect: 5-4-3-2-1 and it went into the charts helped by the weekly plugs.

ABOVE
Promotional photo for
Manfred Mann's single
'Just Like A Woman',
1966

After the moderate success of the follow up Hubble Bubble they hit the big time with the third hit Do Wah Diddy Diddy that featured Jones' vocals brilliantly. It hit number One all over the world notably in the UK and the USA. Now Manfred Mann (or the Manfreds as they became known) were a bona fide part of the British Invasion.

Moving away from their blues base they became poppier and slightly less hard edged, Come Tomorrow and Oh No Not My Baby were definitely in this new mold and If You Gotta Go, Go Now began another string of successes with Dylan written covers.

Pretty Flamingo gave the band a further number one, by which time a solo career beckoned for Jones, he was simply too big by now for the band. Mike D'Abo came in as replacement, various other personnel changes as well saw

ABOVE
Manfred Mann
performing on a
60's TV show

were pretty much forgotten about.

Another Dylan cover gave the D"Abo fronted band their first hit: Just Like a Woman and two more trippy sounding songs-Semi detached Suburban Mr. Jones and Ha Ha said the Clown both charted but it was the next Dylan cover The Mighty Quinn that provided the band with their next number One dominating the charts in spring 1968. Three more hits followed over the next year including Fox on the Run, which they played on Crackerjack-a long way from the Delta blues indeed.

At the end of the 60's the band broke up and pretty much everyone associated went on to do more, Klaus illustrated Beatles' covers and played with the Plastic Ono Band, Tom McGuiness became McGuiness Flint and Manfred was Blinded by the Light with his Earthband. Meanwhile both D'Abo and Jones presented radio shows, wrote more songs and Jones, in particular, kept the Blues flame burning.

Jack Bruce and then Klaus Voormann on bass and Tom McGuiness move to guitar. At the same time they changed record labels (to Fontana) and the hits kept coming, although by now the blues

❝Moving away from their blues base they became poppier and slightly less hard edged, Come Tomorrow and Oh No not my Baby were definitely in this new mold❞

The Moody Blues

The Moody Blues personified, if it was possible, how British music moved from Blues to Pop to Rock over the course of a decade. They started out in Birmingham as a pretty much full throttle blues outfit, transformed themselves into a pop act and then reinvented themselves as a concept album prog rock outfit playing with orchestras and writing some brilliant songs en route. They also marked the change over from a group reliant on singles to become a true album based band.

Ray Thomas, John Lodge and Michael Pinder had been in a local band but had to stop when John Lodge was required to attend college. They recruited Graeme Edge and Denny Laine and with Clint Warwick the five appeared as the Moody Blues for the first time in May 1964. They signed with a local management company who got them a recording contract and their second single in February 1965 hit it big . It was called Go Now, a blues based piano classic Laine had found on a fairly obscure Bessie Banks record. He made it his own.

But management troubles and a failure to follow up this success left the Moodies in disarray. Laine quit in 1966 after a string of under achieving records. The MB's were set to join the ranks of one hit wonders. Until that is John Lodge (the schoolboy from before) and his friend Justin Hayward joined the band replacing Laine and Warwick. (Laine went on to become one third of Wings where he performed Go Now with Macca).

Now they were a different proposition and in November 1966 the band officially reformed and decided to forget the blues covers and novelty records and go for their own compositions. They were helped by Decca, their label, who wanted to launch a new Hi Fi label named Deram with "prog/classical" content. The band also owed a fair bit of cash to the label, so a deal was struck whereby the Moodies would record a rock version of the New World Symphony with an orchestra. Peter Knight was put in charge of the project and the band secured artistic control of their contributions.

The result was Days of Future Passed, a sort of concept album based on the idea of a day in the life of someone who passes through a string of experiences which are highlighted in song-with the two classic examples being the eternal Tuesday Afternoon and Nights in White Satin.

The album was an immediate though qualified success, doing just enough to warrant the effort. But over the years it became more and more successful as "Nights" became a hit again and again

and the album took off in the States. The whole idea of recording with an orchestra had been pinched from The Beatles, as was the use of the Mellotron (which Pinder had shown to the fab four originally). But the mix of strings, early synth, flute and guitars plus Hayward's crystal clear voice was unbeatable. Hayward wrote the two killer tracks but all the band contributed to the writing and production side aided by long time producer Tony Clarke. The mold was set for future success and it became the first of seven consecutive platinum albums.

Next up buoyed by this new direction was the 1968 album In Search of the Lost Chord which included two songs used as singles: Voices in the Sky and Ride my See Saw but singles were no longer the name of the game. As the sixties became the 70's the album became king and On the Threshold of a Dream, To Our Children's Children's Children and A Question of Balance all took them and their audience further away from traditional rock songs and closer to a symphonic form-they even included poetry , sometimes quite a lot of it. They all did really well and the Balance album included Hayward's "Question" a great song. They appeared at the Isle of

Wight in both 69 and 70 which were the classic festivals and cemented the band in the top echelon.

Every Good Boy Deserves Favour and Seventh Sojourn followed and by now with their own label (Threshold based in Cobham) and huge trans continental tours taking months and months with hundreds of roadies and accountants and managers, the band decide to take a break. Pinder in particular who had shouldered a lot of the production burden felt the need for a break. It allowed Lodge and Hayward to get into a simpler more guitar based stride with the Bluejays.

But in 1977 they tried to get back together and recorded the album Octave. In retrospect it all seems a mess as Pinder did not want to tour so the band splintered and the album did not do as well as hoped. They recruited Patrick Moraz to fill the keyboard vacancy and their next album Long Distant Voyager was another Moody style smash. It hit number one in the US album charts.

But really that was their swan song, Moraz left and the other members without Pinder produced a number of other Moody projects, which were all credible, but as the new work became thinner on the ground over the years there were diminishing returns. Now Edge, Hayward and Lodge still tour as the Moody Blues, and sell out huge long US tours, but the days of future passed are just that.

The Move

Like the Moody Blues the Move came from Brum but unlike the Moodies they some-how managed to keep a distinctive midlands character throughout their stay in the UK's charts. Trevor Burton, Ace Kefford, Bev Bevan, Carl Wayne and Roy Wood were the original Move formed in December 1965. They took their name from the fact they all had to move from other bands to join this Midlands super group.

In 1966 managed by Tony Secunda (who also looked after the Moody Blues at the time) they moved to London where they got a residency at the Marquee. They played mainly covers of Byrds or other US group's songs until Secunda managed to persuade Wood to begin writing in his time off. Wood said he could do that-and he could rather well as it turned out. The Move signed a contract and on they went with Secunda doing all he could to get media coverage and airplay. They signed the contract on the back of a topless model for example. Classy.

First single was Night of Fear and it went top three. Like all of their singles it came from Roy Wood and had an undeni-able hook and was full of energy.

The second chart hit featuring Carl Wayne on lead vocals and a still restrained looking Roy Wood on guitar, was I can hear the Grass Grow. It got to number 5 in April 1967 and is apparently something to do with drugs, but who knows? It was

the 60's. Keeping to the gardening theme the first record played on Radio I was the follow up-Flowers in the Rain for which poor Roy Wood never got any royalties after their manager lost a court case to Prime Minister Harold Wilson. It was yet another Secunda publicity stunt involving postcards, some rude allegations and the Labour prime minister. All royalties (even after Wilson's death) were impounded so as a result The Move sacked Secunda and got instead the quiet restrained management of Don Arden on board who had just sold the Small Faces for a brown paper bag full of cash or so the story goes.

Anyway The Move continued to chart-more Wood compositions and ever more bizarre outfits followed: Fire Brigade and their most commercial Blackberry Way both did well and they toured. One package had them; the Nice, Pink Floyd and Jimi Hendrix all on the same bill for under a pound a ticket. How things have changed. They also played the first Isle of Wight festival in 1968. But success in the US was notable by its absence and by the end of the decade Carl Wayne decided he was on his way. He could see that Roy Wood had bigger fish to fry, in the shape of ELO, and soon after Jeff Lynne joined the band.

Brontosaurus was the final hit of this era, Tonight and Chinatown scraped into the charts followed two years later by California Man in May 1972, which marked the band's final chart entry. By now Lynne and Wood had their eyes firmly on the ELO future.

Peter and Gordon

Peter and Gordon first met at the private boys' establishment Westminster School; Asher the son of a Harley Street doctor was a child actor appearing in films often with his sister Jane. Fortunately for Peter and Gordon Jane had a very famous boyfriend indeed and he came to live at the Asher house when his group enjoyed some success in the music industry and he moved down from Liverpool.

Having Paul McCartney as your lodger clearly had some benefits - chiefly that he could knock off a million seller or two for you almost in his sleep. Peter and Gordon had tried singing together, accompanied by their own guitars, and it worked. With Paul's first song for them World Without Love they received loads of attention and it went straight to number one not just in the UK but everywhere. It was a great song funnily enough.

They became a part of that British Invasion but fuelled by McCartney songs they were bound to succeed. Nobody I Know and I Don't Want To See You Again all hit the charts, doing even better in the States than in the UK, Paul tried using a pseudonym to see if sales were effected and under the name Bernard Webb he gave them a song called Woman. It went top twenty both sides of the Atlantic.

In all they had 14 hits in the US, 7 of which did the business at home, their last hit in the UK being Lady Godiva.

"Fuelled by McCartney songs they were bound to succeed"

After the first bout of madness in the 60's finished Asher worked for Paul at Apple where he helped run the record label, in particular working with the young folk singer James Taylor. He stayed with Taylor after Apple's demise managing him in the US to huge stardom and also looking after Linda Ronstadt. I had the pleasure of meeting Asher a couple of times in New York at his huge office overlooking Broadway when he was an executive at Sony, and very nice he was too as you would expect of a Westminster boy.

Gordon was nice too, and sadly he died of a heart attack in 2009 after the duo had got back together again for some special concerts. He was 64. Together in those halcyon days they were innocent, bright eyed and polite with clear well pronounced vocals and some great songs. They showed that the Beatles really did have the power to make anyone famous and sometimes did-ask Peter, or Mary Hopkin, Billy J., Badfinger or James Taylor. Or even Ringo come to that.

Pink Floyd

Pink Floyd rather like Fleetwood Mac became best known after the 60's for being a band rather different to the one they started out as. But whereas Fleetwood Mac had just two main styles, the Floyd are now into their third leader. In the 60's their main man was the crazy diamond himself glittering Syd Barrett.

Syd was more than just a crazy though. He was super talented, charming and charismatic. He was really called Roger, and loved books and drawing. He got a guitar and he loved that too. He loved the Beatles and saw the Rolling Stones and loved them. While still at home in Cambridge with his mate Dave Gilmour Syd began playing small gigs and writing songs. He then moved to North London where he went to Art College like his other great mate Storm.

Meanwhile a group of slightly (but not much) more serious young men who were thinking of being architects called Roger Waters, Nick Mason and Rick Wright were creating a band and living in North London. Syd (really Roger) knew Roger and moved in. Soon he was part of their band, and by 1965 he was the sort of leader and main guitarist. He wrote some more songs and they were simply amazing. Great tunes, hooks, room for spacey sounds and strange intriguing lyrics. Rick was brilliant on keyboards, Nick was a good drummer and the other Roger had something threatening and was very clever too. They were a special bunch that was for sure.

Syd dreamt up the band's name when the one they were using (The Tea Set) was discovered to have already been taken. He put together two blues' men's names: Pink Anderson and Floyd Council. Anderson Council didn't work for him.

They got a residency at an all night venue, which meant playing for hours at a time. They realised that they could stretch out the songs by playing long improvisations and to keep the audience with them they introduced light shows. Pete Jenner a lecturer at the LSE spotted them and signed them up to his newly founded company with Andrew King. Their

connections helped the Floyd whose support amongst the "London Underground" was gaining by the day.

Barrett was in his element, leaping around on stage, wearing cloaks and face paint, looking moody and electric at the same time. He wrote more songs, enough to fill an album. They were great. Eccentric, very English, naïve yet knowing, dreamy and childlike -they set the tone for the time and reflected a mood.

As 1967 began the record companies began to take notice, EMI were at the front of the queue, and the Floyd went into the studio to record a demo. It was a track called Arnold Layne, a Barrett original. It was released and despite some radio stations banning it because of its' interesting theme, it still made it to number 20. It was the story of a man who stole clothes from washing lines, no wonder stations banned it - how subversive!

The follow up See Emily Play released in June of that year pressed exactly the right button. It peaked at number 6 and the band appeared on Top of the Pops.

Next came their first album-named after chapter seven of Wind in the Willows, Piper at the Gates of Dawn was an iconic 60's moment, a creative and intriguing offering that took rock in a new and totally unexpected direction. From now on literally there was no limit to what could be achieved or tried. The gates were now open for artists to push their talent as far as it would take them.

Barrett has to take a lot of the credit but the other three were amazingly open minded, understood what they trying to do and pushed in the same direction. Best of all they were brave enough to try anything. Piper has been a hit re-released every decade since. The front cover has a suitably psychedelic LSD influenced photo of the band wearing kaftans and scarves using a wide angle lens the photographer borrowed from George Harrison, the back has a Syd drawing on it. He wrote eight of the tracks and co-wrote two others.

By the time the album came out Syd was already pretty much spent. The acid was getting to him, the tales are sad and numerous. Within a year he was gone, Dave Gilmour came into the Floyd at first to bolster up the group but eventually to replace Syd. Roger stood up as a songwriter and with Mason, Wright and Gilmour delivered Saucerful of Secrets, and then Ummagumma that contained the last vestige of Syd-the live version of Astronomy Domine.

Pink Floyd might not have had the greatest effect on the charts of the 60's, but on every year that followed they were there alongside the Beatles and very few others as the founding fathers of our new culture.

Procol Harum

Procol Harum had two hit singles in the 60's both in 1967, one was the sombre Hombur, the other was one of the most iconoclastic songs of the decade, A Whiter Shade of Pale and if they had never recorded another song in their existence this alone would have been enough to write Procul Harum into the pantheon of rock legends. It is a genuine rock classic.

The song became their debut single and went to number one where it stayed for six weeks before being displaced by All You Need is Love. It topped the charts during the summer of love, and surely stands for far more than just a four minute long pop song.

Those Bach influenced organ chords first rang out in Olympic Studios in Barnes (now a hip cinema) where the band-Gary Brooker keyboards and lead vocals, Mathew Fisher on Hammond Organ, lyricist Keith Reid, David Knights on bass and Ray Royer on guitar were creating their first album. It was released on Decca's Deram label on May 12 1967 with Lime Street Blues as the b side. Compositional credits were down to Brooker and Reid (who provided the mind bending lyrics.) It was produced by Denny Cordell who also cut the Joe Cocker number One With a Little Help from My Friends amongst a slew of credits.

The record instantly became a conver-

> **"This alone would have been enough to write Procul Harum into the pantheon of rock legends"**

musical composer's royalties. To date it has shipped over 10 million units, one of just a handful of songs to have sold so many.

The song is certainly unusual; it is long for a single at 4.03 but only contains two verses, and a title that had previously not been in the vernacular. There are in existence two other verses, which seem to confirm the nautical nature of the song, full of marine allusions and effectively likening sex with an unknown partner to being at sea. But with tarot references, and words like fandango involved who really knows. And who cares as well, it is exactly the kind of lyrical content that can mean different things to different listeners, Ambiguous, resonant, playful, crazy and intriguing. It's the sixties in one song.

They were a cool looking band too, and the po-faced Homburg was similarly ambiguous and other worldly. In the 70's they made some records with orchestras and created some good songs but nothing would ever touch Whiter Shade of Pale, it's been voted best single of the decade, it's been in movies, it sums up a time, an expression and a mood.

sation piece-what did it mean, what was the symbolism, who were the band and was it really a classical record by Bach? The mystery surrounding its' meaning is part of the attraction and in truth the record was still causing waves 40 years later when the compositional rights were finally sorted out by the Law Lords, who ruled Mathew Fisher (who had added the Bach bits) deserved

The Rolling Stones

There really was only one band to rival the Beatles and that was the Stones. It was a deliberate policy to try and be as different as possible to the fab four and the brain wave came from Andrew Loog Oldham, the man who made the Stones roll.

The Stones began on a Dartford railway platform in Kent when Keith and Mick bumped into each other. Mick was quite posh, the son of a teacher living in smart mock Tudor suburbia. He appeared on Blue Peter demonstrating gymnastics and rock climbing. But when he met Keith he was carrying a clutch of blues records, the hobby of a middle class grammar school-boy en route for university and a nice middle class job.

But Keith took Jagger off on a ride that meant suburbia would never look the same to Mick. Together with Brian Jones, who was the original leader of the band, they were regulars at the Ealing Blues club where they befriended Alexis Korner. They linked up with Charlie Watts and Bill Wyman and started to cover their favourite blues tunes.

To begin with Brian was very much the leader. He even went so far as to offer Manfred Mann's Paul Jones the lead singer role, before he settled on Jagger. He also got most of their early material together and organized a manager- the émigré Giorgio Gomelsky who was a talented, though extremely hip and disorganized individual. Giorgio was all about "the scene" and not

THE ROLLING STONES

so much about contracts. He created the Crawdaddy Club in Richmond, where he caught the mood of the moment. He put the young Stones in as the house band. They played weekends and the queues at the end of the District line opposite the railway station grew and grew, people loved them.

Sure enough it was only a matter of time before the record companies came calling, but so did other hipsters like Andrew Oldham. He was even younger than the Stones, but had already been a publicist for the Beatles. He signed the Stones and promised to make Mick a star. Mick liked the idea.

Pretty soon they had a contract with Decca (trying to make up for that fatal error of missing out on you know who) and a hit record on their hands. They recorded a cover song and then a gift from the Beatles (I Wanna be Your Man) to thank for that. John later said "It was rubbish-well we weren't going to give them anything good were we?"

They recorded at Olympic in Barnes, Mick got a series of great looking girlfriends (first Shrimpton and then Faithful) and Gered Mankowitz took some stunning pictures of the band behind wire. They looked horrible in them, politicians, the police, older schoolteachers, Mary Whitehouse, even some Bishops were upset, TV pundits complained, Would You Let Your Daughter Marry a Rolling Stone? the Oldham inspired tabloids screamed.

The result was Britain's youth was polarised; suddenly they were either Beatles or Stones fans. Clean cut or filthy went the choice. Of course you could like both-I did. And when Oldham locked Mick and Keith in the studio and told them they could not come out until they had written a hit it all got even better. Their first Beatles driven hit went to number 12 after Come On their first record just about charted. But their next Not Fade Away went top three and It's All Over Now hit the top spot in

March 1964. From then until the end of the 60's the Stones went on an eleven record unbroken string of hits, ranging through Little Red Rooster (surely the most roots of any British Blues record to hit number one) to Satisfaction, via The Last Time, Get off of my Cloud, Paint it Black, Jumping Jack Flash and Honky Tonk Women.

The history of the Stones reads like a history of Britain's counter culture. Glamorous, sordid, drug riddled, talented, death laden and threatening. They embraced it all and they made the world their stage. Altamont to Hyde Park, society parties to being caught urinating behind a petrol station, they did it all. There were casualties, there were disasters and there were triumphs, After all it was only rock 'n' roll, but we loved it. Forty years later on they have not radically increased their catalogue of great songs, the albums have become more treasured, but it is as a live act that we worship them now.

Ronnie has come in, Bill's not playing with them, Brian, of course, has passed away and Mick Taylor came and went, but Jagger and Richard seem to be able to last forever. Keith in particular has an indestructible quality and a sense of humour that can conquer any situation and boy does he find

himself in some situations. They still court death and mayhem but then that is what being in the Stones is all about. Long may it all last, they carry the spirit of the 60's in every ounce of their beings.

ABOVE
Ronnie Wood (left) and
Mick Jagger (right)

Sandie Shaw

Sandra Godrich was born in Dagenham on February 26 1947 and like thousands of her generation went to work in the Ford factory down the road. But Sandie occasionally did a bit of modeling, and crucially sang in a talent show where she was spotted by Adam Faith. He put her in touch with his manager Eve Taylor and while still just 16 years old Sandie had a new name, a recording contract with Pye and was teamed up with hit songwriter Chris Andrews.

Their first effort was not a hit but Taylor then turned to the tried and tested, a cover of the Bacharach/David song Always Something there to Remind Me. It hit the charts in October 1964 ending up at the very top; it was Sandie's first number one.

Always slightly eccentric Sandie refused to wear shoes and on TV she cut a glamorous stylish figure with her razor sharp fringe, long legs and mascara. She personified the 60's swinging image as seen round the world and although not stellar successes her records all entered the Billboard hot 100.

Next up was an Andrews's composition Girl Don't Come that also went top five, as did the first release of 1965 I'll Stop at Nothing. Three more hits followed that year including her next number one Long Live Love. Andrews, who was from nearby Romford, wrote

❝Always slightly eccentric Sandie refused to wear shoes and on TV she cut a glamorous stylish figure with her razor sharp fringe, long legs and mascara. She personified the 60's swinging image❞

some 16 songs for Sandie and even had time to have a hit himself (Yesterday Man). The formula just kept on working with Andrews, Taylor and Shaw producing and Sandie's place in the top division alongside Cilla, Dusty and Lulu assured - but the best was still to come.

In 1966 despite five more chart hits the sales were showing signs of declining. Taylor thought about moving Shaw to a more middle of the road position with cabaret beckoning, but along came Eurovision in 1967 and Sandie had her biggest hit. Performing five songs on the Rolf Harris show Sandie ended up singing a Coulter/Martin composition called Puppet on a String in Vienna. She wasn't particularly keen on it, remarking that it was not her style of music. But it seemed to be everyone else's as the song won by the biggest every margin, the

contest was a massive TV event and the disc sold bucket loads. It gave Sandie her biggest number one and cemented her position in popular culture. The barefoot princess of pop reigned supreme for one year at least.

The following year Sandie combined her marriage to Jeff Banks and her love of fashion by setting up her own fashion label, and moved into TV more, appearing as a regular on light entertainment shows including a series of her own. But as the 70's took hold Sandie appeared less, the chart hits dried up and she only resurfaced when The Smiths got in touch and she recorded some of their material. She officially retired in 2013 but with over 20 chart entries and that golden moment of Eurovision when she became our first ever winner, Sandie's place amongst the top echelon by then was confirmed.

The Searchers

Named after a John Ford 1956 movie starring John Wayne The Searchers could claim for some time to be second only to their fellow Liverpudlians, the Beatles, in the pantheon of best British group, with five smash hits in the 15 months after their first number one Sweets for my Sweet in June 63. With their suits and fringes they were very much of their time and alongside the fab four, Billy J., Gerry and Cilla were at the very forefront of the Mersey sound on the covers of a hundred magazines and appearing every week on Thank Your Lucky Stars.

The band was made up of Chris Curtis, Mike Pender, John McNally, and Tony Jackson and like the fab four they played in the Star Club, Hamburg and The Cavern. They signed for Pye with Tony Hatch as producer and Sweets for My Sweet hit number one. They were in the forefront of the British Invasion and in all had ten hits in the US.

But it was at home that they struck gold with Sugar and Spice, Needles and Pins and Don't Throw Your Love Away all enjoying levels of success normally associated only with the Beatles.

The chart successes kept coming for the next two years, they appeared on Ed Sullivan and topped the bill throughout the UK. In all 15 hits came from the band during this time including classics like When You Walk in the Room, What have they Done

"With five smash hits in the 15 months after their first number one, Sweets for my Sweet"

The Searches touch down, 17th September 1965

to the Rain and Love Potion No. 9 with their vocal harmonies and driving guitar sound providing a consistent and almost ever present backbeat in the top twenty.

But label changes, personnel issues and one fatal flaw contributed to their lack of lasting power. The flaw was that the group was not producing new material themselves and reliant on cover versions they inevitably fell behind the Beatles and The Stones who were effectively delivery vehicles for the bands writers. Chris Curtis was the closest the Searchers had to a consistent writer (and he was a good pr/front man)

But as the hits dried up Curtis left the band in 1966 and put together the musicians who became Deep Purple. Sadly he did not actually play in Deep Purple despite putting them together leaving Richie Blackmore, Jon Lord and co to get on with world domination without him. Meanwhile he quite sensibly preferred to take a job with the Inland Revenue in 1969 and stayed a taxman for a further 19 years.

The Searchers with versions featuring both John McNally and Mike Pender are still out there somewhere. They are carrying the banner for the Mersey Sound they helped to create 50 years ago, and had so much success with.

Small Faces

The Small Faces inspired a generation, and not just the Britpoppers, with their r'n'b infused power pop centred around one of the 60's greatest vocalists and writers "Little" Stevie Marriott, but then the rest of the band were pretty good as well. Kenney Jones on drums, Ronnie "Plonk" Lane, co-writer and bassist and Ian McLagan on keys completed a line-up that whether in this form or later as just the Faces with Rod were simply unstoppable on their day.

Lane and Marriott met in a music shop in 1965 in Manor Park. They listened to records together, got playing and hit it off. They recruited Jones and then after a false start with Jimmy Winston got "Mac" on keys. They were Faces-all mod wise guys, and they were small, so the name was a good one. They shared a love of the blues and singers like Otis Redding, Bobby Bland and the rest. But right from the start they wrote songs together, with Ronnie Lane's love of melody and Marriott able to belt out a tune with a unique and soulful voice.

They signed a contract to manager Don Arden and he got them hooked up with Decca. With their unique, quirky lyrics and hook laden melodies the hits kept coming for four glorious years from Whatcha Gonna Do About It in 1964 through to The Universal in summer 1968. All or Nothing hit number

One during the World Cup summer in August 66, it summed up a mood, a time and a place and was immediately before they started to tinker with psychedelia visiting Itchycoo Park and beyond.

They appealed at first to the mods in the audience, but gradually they embraced a wider audience, as did The Who. Sha la la la Lee allowed Marriott to indulge his powerful vocals, Hey Girl had a catchy swirling Hammond organ sound, All or Nothing took them in a new direction confirmed by My Minds' Eye which was essentially a demo released as they were splitting with Arden. All were hits.

The split with Don Arden came over money of course-which for some reason always seemed to allude the group. Arden then proceeded to sell them to Andrew Oldham who put them on the hip Immediate Label he had formed. They set up camp in Olympic Studios in Barnes and took their music even further towards psychedelia. With their firm mastery of roots blues style they had the confidence to experiment. Here Comes the Nice in June 1967 was their first effervescent single that sparked into the charts, it was followed by their finest hour Itchycoo

Park, Tin Soldier (featuring Marriott's latest squeeze PP Arnold on vocals) and then the brilliant album Ogden's Nut Gone Flake with The Universal, Afterglow, Long Ago's and Far away and Lazy Sunday as stand out tracks amongst many great songs and delicious linking material courtesy of Professor Stanley Unwin.

They never played the album live, which was a tragedy as it stopped them crossing the bridge into "more serious" material like The Who managed. The result was they were still labeled as a pop band in Marriott's mind who in frustration quit Small Faces at the end of 1968 more or less at their peak.

He went on to form Humble Pie with Peter Frampton before his tragically early death in a home fire. The other three joined forces with Rod Stewart and as The Faces became the UK's biggest band before Lane quit to go solo, ahead of a terrible time and ultimate death at the hands of MS. Kenny Jones joined the Who for a while, and Ian McLagan was never short of a piano stool-he worked with lots of different acts and settled in the US.

Marriott and Lane are still sadly missed.

The Spencer Davis Group

Welsh guitarist Spencer Davis started the group in Birmingham in 1963 when he recruited the two Winwood brothers Muff and Stevie to join him in a new blues based band. Along with Pete York they gigged around Brum until the following year when Chris Blackwell saw them and signed them to his new Island Records label. He produced them himself.

With Stevie's voice based on Ray Charles and the blues licks just right, the Group were as good a blues outfit in the UK at the time as anyone. They blended the soulful sound of Winwood, which had a great hard edge for someone so young (he was barely 14 when he first joined the band) with a cool organ, driving rumbling bass and solid guitar sound.

Their second single hit the top spot in December 1965. Keep on Runnin' was a cover of a Jackie Edwards song, but you would never have guessed it, they made it completely their own. It was the closest the UK had come to having a full-blown blues record at number one.

For the follow up the following year in April they chose another Edwards' track Somebody Help Me. It too went straight to number one. They completed the trilogy with When I come Home which did less well but by now they were firmly established on the music scene.

At the end of the year they moved up a gear with two self-composed hits, both classics: first off in November Gimme Some Lovin' followed in February 1967 by I'm a Man. Both have had endless cover versions (best by The Blues Brothers and Chicago respectively in my opinion) but by any definition they are great songs.

Muff Winwood was by now looking to move more into production and he did so under Blackwell's wing at Island where he scored loads more hits.

Meanwhile Little Stevie moved on to form the brilliant Traffic, a psychedelic super group that had Paper Sun, Hole in My Shoe and Here we go round the Mulberry Bush as their first three singles. Stevie then left to form Blind Faith with Eric Clapton, Ric

Gretsch and Ginger Baker before doing another stint with Traffic and kicking off a long lasting solo career with huge hits on both sides of the Atlantic.

The Spencer Davis Group still goes out on the road from time to time with Spencer who lives in the USA now.

Tom Jones

Tom Jones has sold over 100 million records, has topped the bill in Vegas, become a knight of the realm and has had at the time of writing 36 top 40 records in the UK ranging in style from Prince's Kiss to The Green Green Grass of Home. He is without doubt the most successful male solo singer of the last 50 years and his style runs from country to show standards, blues to soul and rock.

But it is as a soul and blues singer that he started out on the rocky road. Tom was born Thomas Jones Woodward on June 7 1940 in Pontypridd, Glamorgan, where he sang in choirs, at church and at family gatherings like a number of his local compatriots. At 12 Jones was smitten with TB and had to spend two years recovering. He spent a lot of time listening to the Blues artists from the US and when he was better he started to perform their numbers.

But life was not smooth; he married his girlfriend at the age of 16 when she became pregnant and worked in a glove factory and then on building sites to keep the young family going. He continued to sing in the pubs and clubs, with a beat combo, but despite a false start or two he eventually got his break. His full throttle baritone was heard by music manager Gordon Mills who changed Tom Woodward to Tom Jones and moved him to London.

> **"His full throttle baritone was heard by music manager Gordon Mills who changed Tom Woodward to Tom Jones and moved him to London"**

Mills sorted out a recording contract with Decca and a single appeared-to no response. So Mills picked up a Les Reed song he co-wrote with him called It's Not Unusual. Tom recorded a demo intending that Sandie Shaw would record the final version. But Sandie loved what she heard and suggested they put it out with Tom's vocal and she would pass on it.

The result was a huge worldwide hit, that went to number one in the UK and the tune became Tom's signature song. He simply can't leave the stage without his army of fans demanding it so they can throw their panties to him as it ends. I've seen it happen, it's true.

Three more hits swiftly followed then What's New Pussycat? and Thunderball crashed into the charts, followed by Green Green Grass of Home (another number one) and I'm Coming Home, the ultra camp Delilah (check the Alex Harvey version), Help Yourself, and Love Me Tonight,. Every year after Unusual in February 1965 for the rest of the

decade Tom had a minimum of two or three top ten hits. He was unstoppable.

As the sixties became the seventies Tom became more of an international star, he made international TV series, did huge international tours and became friends with Elvis, played weeks at Vegas, did TV specials with people like Raquel Welch and gradually as we moved into the 80's (especially after the death of Gordon Mills) Tom's popularity at home seemed to be dipping.

But with son Mark at the helm and Tom choosing some great songs he enjoyed a huge resurgence of appeal. He sang Prince's Kiss, appeared at Glastonbury and became hip again especially after some carefully thought through collaborations.

Now Tom's status could not be higher, he is prime inter pares with the rock aristocracy, a regular on top rating TV shows and has developed a shrewd line in self-deprecatory humour. Plus he can still blast out that golden voice. It's not unusual it's unique.

Wayne Fontana and the Mindbenders

In 1963 Manchester singer Wayne Fontana (real name Glyn Ellis born October 1945) needed a backing band. He recruited Bob Lang Ric Rothwell and Eric Stewart and Wayne Fontana and the Mindbenders were born. Wayne had named himself after Elvis' drummer and The Mindbenders took their name from a Dirk Bogarde film-lucky it wasn't Darling they saw at the Regent that week.

Of course there was only one label he could be on-not Wayne Records but Fontana- and they released the cover version of Um Um Um Um Um Um the Major Lance song written by Curtis Mayfield. Lance's version was big in the USA but in the UK it was Wayne's that hit the top ten making it to number 5 in October 1964.

His follow up did even better Game of Love written by Clint Ballard (who also wrote You're No Good-check the Linda Ronstadt version) hit number 2 in the UK and topped the charts in the US, now Wayne was part of the British invasion knocking Freddie and the Dreamers off the top spot before Herman's Hermits

"Wayne had named himself after Elvis' drummer"

took over. The Game of Love hit number one in April 1965.

But that was about to become it for Wayne as the Mindbenders left him citing personality clashes. Well the story is that Wayne actually left them storming off stage shouting, "that's it", during a US tour. He continued as a solo act but things went from bad to worse for him- his last single Pamela Pamela was his most successful hitting number 11 in the UK but after that…nothing but a long time without a hit, followed by bankruptcy and illness. Otherwise all fine.

Meanwhile The Mindbenders kept going, especially in the US where they played a number of topline tours. Eric Stewart became the singer and they recorded A Groovy Kind of Love, their first without Wayne.

Written by Toni Wine and Carole Bayer Sager (who was later to marry and write with Burt Bacharach) it was massive for the Mindbenders hitting number 2 in the UK and number 1 in the States in January 1966 just like the Game of Love had done. They instantly

RIGHT
Wayne Fontana &
The Mindbenders,
18th September 1965

set off on a massive US tour and another Wine/Bayer Sager number Ashes to Ashes got into the top twenty.

They wrote a concept album, supported James Brown across the US and appeared in To Sir with Love but the Mindbenders did not have a hit again as such. However things didn't finish there for Stewart.

In 1968 Graham Gouldman joined the band for its last few months and it wasn't long before he and Stewart formed one of the greatest bands of the 70's the brilliant 10cc. They first hit the charts again as

Hot Legs and then set up Strawberry Studios teaming up with Kevin Godley and Lol Crème to record some of the wittiest and catchiest pop tunes ever written. Although only together in this form for a short period 10cc continue to have a profound effect on the industry and Graham Gouldman's 10cc are still a major force on the road and at festivals around the globe.

Meanwhile A Groovy Kind of Love became a classic cemented by an inferior though bigger selling worldwide number one version by Phil Collins in 1988.

"They wrote a concept album, supported James Brown across the US and appeared in To Sir with Love"

The Tremeloes

The Tremeloes started their musical life in the mid 50's when still at school. East End boys living in Barking Brian Poole, Alan Blakley, Alan Howard, Rick West, and Dave Munden were all in their early teens and knocked out a nice line in Buddy Holly covers and rock songs. Brian started out as a guitarist but moved to lead singer and they became known as Brian Poole and the Tremeloes.

Life changed for them in 1962 when on New Years Day they auditioned for Decca Records. They were up against a quartet from Liverpool, but they won the record contract and Decca rejected the Beatles. Ironically a cover of Twist and Shout (which became indelibly linked with the fab four) was their first chart entry reaching the top five. Meanwhile The Beatles managed to get by and got over their disappointment.

In September 1963 their second hit Do You Love Me (which was a thinly veiled re working of Twist and Shout) reached number one. Candy Man, Someone Someone and Three Bells all charted, as did I Want Candy (later a Bow Wow Wow single) but in 1966 there was a change. Poole left to go solo and The Tremeloes rejigged their line up. Len "Chip" Hawkes joined (yes Chesney's Dad) and Howard left.

Little went right for Brian Poole's solo career, but the Trems had a fresh breath of life. Switching to CBS in 1967

they put out a cover of the Cat Stevens' album track Here Comes my Baby, it went top five and was on the charts for six weeks. They followed it with the massive number one Silence is Golden which was their biggest hit and a number one. Both records hit the US top twenty as well.

Even the Bad Times are Good, Suddenly You Love Me, and Call me Number One were the highlights as they continued to plunder the charts right up to November 1969 when with the mood change in record buying the Trems started the inevitable descent. Blakley and Hawkes wrote some good tunes which kept the band afloat, and they even tried a new "heavy metal" approach which was risible and their last hit was Hello Buddy in 1971.

The Troggs

"You don't hit it like that, hit it like this and sprinkle a bit of fairy dust on it." The Troggs are from Wiltshire, Andover actually, and were originally called The Troglodytes. They don't instantly appear to be rock star material but in Wild Thing and Love is All Around they have created two giant hits that have enhanced and changed the rock canon.

Reg Presley, Chris Britten, Pete Staples and Ronnie Bond were signed by Larry Page, the Kinks' manager and he got them a contract with a couple of record labels when one would have done really. Their first release didn't do much but he then worked with them on a Chip Taylor song Wild Thing and they managed to pull off the definitive recording in a matter of minutes. It is still regarded as one of the foundations of rock recordings. With the most simple of chord progressions,

but with a deceptive guitar tuning, and a solo on an ocarina it has become a classic.

It hit number one in the US on both record labels and in the UK they were massive throughout the summer of 66 following it up immediately with the Presley song With a Girl Like You.

Wild Thing has gone on to become one of the most recorded songs of them all, and the Troggs version along with Jimi Hendrix's remain the ones to match. The Troggs have covered it themselves

a number of times with collaborators ranging from Hurricane Higgins and Oliver Reed to REM (yes live in Athens GA) and Wolf from Gladiators.

But after Wild Thing and "A Girl" they continued to chart: I can't Control Myself also went top three, followed by Anyway that you want Me, Give it to me and Night of the Long Grass. But with the hits drying up in November 1967 they still had one last hurrah saved for last-Love is all Around spent another seven weeks on the chart peaking at number five. Twenty-seven years later in 1994 Wet Wet Wet recorded the song for the soundtrack to Four weddings and a Funeral. It went to number one and stayed there for 15 weeks.

The writing royalties for this made Reg Presley temporarily a very rich man, but he gave most of it away to research for UFO's (which are big in Wiltshire what with all those crop circles and all). Good luck to him.

Sadly both Presley and Bond are no longer with us, but the Troggs continued to stay in the Andover area despite all their global success. They conquered the charts and managed to sprinkle a bit of magic dust wherever they were heard.

The Who

Wildly chaotic and anarchic, The Who are the most dynamic act that rock has yet produced and during their heyday which was probably around 1971-8 the group was a genuine maelstrom of energy, both destructive and creative, and a package of personalities that was always on the verge of exploding. If you were lucky enough to see them live at the Isle of Wight, the Rainbow, Charlton, The Oval or at the University of Leeds you simply knew you were in the presence of a phenomena unrivalled on planet Earth. I was that lucky and went every night of their run in 1971 at the Rainbow and I can say without fear of contradiction that the members of the group created the most perfect live act it is possible to imagine.

Four diverse personalities made up the band, one a great songwriter and artistic spirit but with enough angst to fill a stadium, alongside him a vocalist who could live those songs. Pete wrote for Roger and Roger grabbed those songs and made them come alive, he could hold a massive crowd in his hand. Then at the back the solid Ox, a musical power house and a dark force, John Entwistle. For good measure throw in the greatest rock drummer yet, with a unique technique, a wicked sense of humour, a super fast intelligence, a bag of explosives and a musical style that was completely his own-the incomparable Keith Moon. Together on

their day they were simply as good, as loud, as tuneful and as exciting as it gets.

Their success was built on the solid core of Townshend's amazing output as a writer. But that was yet to be realised when the elements of the band started to come together.

The three founding members-John, Pete and Roger were all West London grammar school boys. Bright but slightly rough they lived in Acton, around the White City estate before the BBC and Westfield's shopping centre had poshed it all up. It was a tough part of London. John played classical music as well as rock, Pete became an art student (yes another one joining Lennon, McCartney, Clapton, Ray Davies and a host of oth-

"You simply knew you were in the presence of a phenomena"

ers who came from Art to rock), while Roger quit school early and worked as a labourer. He also formed a band-the Detours and got the other two to play in it.

They performed in pubs and drinking clubs, they did weddings and parties; Roger was the leader and looked after the cash. The Detours was a five piece with Daltrey playing guitar as well as singing, but gradually members fell away and Pete became the only guitarist. Lets face it he was good enough.

In 1964 they had a regular gig at the Oldfield Hotel in Greenford and while there they met a new young drummer who liked the idea of joining them. They were on the look out for a new one so auditioned him. Typically part of the kit got broken while he attacked the drums but the audition was a success, The Who were born. During the year under the guidance of mod PR and pill popper Pete Meaden The Who became a mod group, and their following grew. Called briefly The High Numbers (a Meaden idea) the band got a single out called I'm the Face but it did not make it. It was The Who that had the following not the High Numbers.

They parted ways with Meaden, and signed for Kit Lambert and Chris Stamp (Terence's brother) and the change was instant. Lambert spotted them in the Railway Hotel in Harrow and was mesmerised. He and Stamp were actually filmmakers and planned to make a movie about the band but first they made them worldwide stars. A few lucky co-incidences helped them on their way.

First off they changed their repertoire and Pete came more to the fore. Their new managers encouraged him to write songs, they also filmed their gig at the Railway Hotel in Wealdstone, and it was while playing there that Townshend accidentally, at first, and then on purpose started breaking his guitar into bits.

The result was electric; the auto destruct art happening that they spun on this became their signature, and singled them out.

Now they needed a hit and another chance helped: Lambert and Stamp contacted Shel Talmy, the man behind the Kinks' hits and as fate would have it Dave Davies had just started ripping his amplifier to bits while creating the unique chords that make up You Really Got Me.

It hit the spot for Pete who immediately penned I Can't Explain, and the first single for The Who was there for the taking.

Talmy licensed it to Decca and it came out on Brunswick, the Decca label for US acts (Talmy was an American) and helped by a performance on Ready Steady Go and the mod following the record climbed the charts ending up at number eight in April 1965. They immediately followed it up with Anyway Anyhow Anywhere which was an attempt to try and catch the live sound they were creating. It performed at the same level as Can't Explain but their next single was the game changer.

Originally much slower and sonorous, Pete re-arranged his song about teenage anger and alienation, the electrified My Generation charged up the charts and with Roger's stuttering vocals sounded like nothing else out there. The song also gave the band a unique opportunity to feature all four members in equal measures- those vocals, a bass solo, the amazing drum breaks and Pete's guitar style melded into one classic, incomparable track. In November it entered the charts, went to number two and was still there two months later. In the US it dented the 100 but it was not until I can See for Miles that the US re-ally bought Who singles. A TV appearance on The Smothers Brothers resulted in explosions, bits of drum kit flying about the studio and Pete getting a burst ear drum.

The Who were now in their pomp. Daltrey and Townshend famously fell out big time, Daltrey lost control of the group after being sacked and then re-instated over the row. The band now functioned democratically and their managers got rid of Talmy too. The next single Substitute was on Track records, their own label. They followed it with I'm a Boy, Happy Jack, Pictures of Lily, I can see for Miles and Pinball Wizard. They had joined the top league on the peaks occupied only by the Stones, Beatles and Kinks.

The rest is part of rock folklore. Pete wrote Tommy and the Who moved from being a singles band to becoming the greatest rock band on earth, an albums artist, and certainly the best live act. They followed Tommy with Who's Next and then Quadrophenia, they made films, they toured and then sadly Moon died and they were never quite the same of course. Now with John gone, they are still special but for those crucial years in 1969 to 1978 they were the best, a massive influence on everyone who heard or saw them.

The Yardbirds

The Yardbirds are the premier guitar band known to man. If you look at any list of the greatest rock guitarists then this band had three of them: Eric Clapton, Jeff Beck and Jimmy Page, and their influence on the music landscape is still evident for all to see.

They started off as a blues based combo in South West London centred on Paul Samwell Smith, Chris Dreja, Jim McCarty and lead vocalist Keith Relf along with early member Top Topham. They formed in May 63 and in September of that year replaced the Rolling Stones as the house band at the Crawdaddy Club in Richmond.

They were art students at Kingston Art College, where Eric Clapton was as well. Top Topham was young; in fact too young according to his parents, for the rock n roll lifestyle so in October 1963 the

band turned to Eric. The Yardbirds were bright, and serious scholars of the Chicago blues. They played authentic blues music, with that Richmond/Twickenham twist and they instantly created a following.

They had the Stones' original manager Giorgio Gomelsky as their mentor and he set about promoting them. He gave Eric the nickname "slowhand" due to the audience giving him a slow hand clap when changing strings, and he built up their following and got them a recording contract.

To start with their repertoire was es-

sentially Blues classics such as Smoke-
stack Lightning, Boom Boom, and
Good Morning Little School Girl. They
introduced a whole new audience to the
Blues and with the Stones created an
atmosphere where the actual Blues legends themselves felt able to visit Britain
and play. John Lee Hooker popped up
on Ready Steady Go and Sonny Wil-
liamson toured with The Yardbirds and
their first album Five Live Yardbirds
reflects this authentic Blues repertoire.
Check out Eric's solo on Too Much
Monkey Business, it is lightning fast.

But then for their third single Giorgio
and Paul Samwell Smith got hold of a
song called For Your Love. It was written
by a youngster in Manchester Graham
Gouldman (that's right he became part of
10cc and wrote songs for Herman and the
Hollies). But at this time he was still unknown. His manager told him the song
was so good The Beatles would record it.
Graham was sceptical but the track was
duly sent to the fab four at Hammersmith
Odeon where they were performing their
Christmas Show. Of course they were
OK for songs…but they passed it on
to their support act that just happened
to be The Yardbirds. Giorgio loved it.

For the session the classic harpsichord part came about by chance, Brian Auger was hired to play organ but the studio did not have one booked for the session, so they got the only keyboard in the building-an 18th Century harpsichord- and Auger created the classic sound we all love. The record became a massive hit in both the UK and the USA. It was all too much for poor Eric-commercial success had not been part of the plan and he quit.

Clapton recommended Jimmy Page as a replacement, but Page decided against it for the time being so in turn suggested Jeff Beck. Beck's feedback and distortion effects fitted perfectly into the mood of the time, (as witnessed in the film Blow Up featuring the group) and Eric was hardly missed at all. In fact Eric's suit which he wore when perform- ing with the band fitted Beck perfectly.

For their next single they went straight to Gouldman and he came up with the goods. Heart Full of Soul, again produced by Giorgio but also cred- ited as musically directed by Samwell Smith, had that great fuzzy guitar riff and some lovely echoey vocals. Again it smashed the top ten all over the world.

The Beck era Yardbirds produced some of their finest work: Evil Hearted You (another Gouldman classic), Still I'm Sad, and then the first self penned hit Shapes of Things. All were top five hits and ex- tended the psychedelic influenced, Blues rooted guitar pop brand. They recorded Shapes in late 65 in Chess studios in Chi- cago then finished it off at RCA in Hol- lywood the following year. Again Giorgio Gomelsky is credited as the record's producer, and Samwell Smith is billed as music director and Beck's solo is a classic.

That summer the group recorded The Yardbirds album featuring songs entirely written by themselves and lots of guitar ef- fects. It is a great album but marked the be- ginning of the end of a glorious era and the start of something special. To begin with Samwell Smith left soon after the album was complete, he decided he wanted to become a record producer full time. And he did - most notably with Cat Stevens.

Jimmy Page now did join the band, to start with on bass until Chris Dreja mas- tered it and moved to bass guitar from rhythm where he was replaced by Page alongside Beck. They toured the States with this line up- and it must have been amazing. Happenings Ten Years Time Ago features both of them on record to-

LEFT
Eric Clapton

gether but they made no albums while in tandem. One curio came out of this time though-Jeff Beck's first solo success was Hi Ho Silver Lining and the B side, Beck's Bolero features Page, Beck, John Paul Jones, pianist Nicky Hopkins and Keith Moon on drums- now that is a band which would have been worth half a crown to watch.

In October 1966 Beck was finally sacked from the band after a series of no-shows and missed concerts. The band was now tired and drink and drugs affected. For most of 67 they seemed to be touring the States but disillusion was setting in and new manager Simon Napier Bell failed to inject the band with any commercial success. Dreja wanted to become a photographer (and he did, an excellent one) and Relf and McCarty had other types of music to explore (which they did) until Relf sadly died. Which left Jimmy Page to soldier on with the Yardbirds name for a few more months. In July 68 their last concert held bizarrely in Luton was announced- and Page together with the Yardbirds' new manager Peter Grant set about enlisting some new recruits.

After first approaching Terry Reid, who said no, they got an unknown singer from the midlands called Robert Plant to join with his drummer mate John Bonham and Page persuaded fellow session king John Paul Jones to come in on keyboards and bass guitar. For the next few months they rehearsed and then toured as late as October 1968 as the Yardbirds. Key Yardbirds songs like Dazed and Confused were part of the set but they really took off the following year after a slight name change to Led Zeppelin. What happened next is well known. If just that single fact was all you knew about the Yardbirds it would be enough to explain why the group are one of the most influential in the story of rock.

Design & Artwork: ALEX YOUNG

Published by: DEMAND MEDIA LIMITED

Publisher: JASON FENWICK

Written by: ROBIN BEXTOR